KING RICHARD
THE SECOND

WILLIAM SHAKESPEARE

1st WORLD
LIBRARY
Literary Society

KING RICHARD THE SECOND

WILLIAM SHAKESPEARE

© 1st World Library - Literary Society, 2005
PO Box 2211
Fairfield, IA 52556
www.1stworldlibrary.org
First Edition

LCCN: 2005927915
Softcover ISBN: 1-4218-1364-5
Hardcover ISBN: 1-4218-1326-2
eBook ISBN: 1-4218-1402-1

Purchase *"King Richard The Second"*
as a traditional bound book at:
www.1stWorldLibrary.org/purchase.asp?ISBN=1-4218-1364-5

1st World Library Literary Society is a nonprofit organization dedicated to promoting literacy by:

Creating a free internet library accessible from any computer worldwide.
Hosting writing competitions and offering book publishing scholarships.

Readers interested in supporting literacy
through sponsorship, donations or
membership please contact:
literacy@1stworldlibrary.org
Check us out at: www.1stworldlibrary.org
and start downloading free ebooks today.

King Richard The Second
contributed by the Charles Family
in support of
1st World Library Literary Society

DRAMATIS PERSONAE

KING RICHARD THE SECOND

JOHN OF GAUNT, Duke of Lancaster - uncle to the King

EDMUND LANGLEY, Duke of York - uncle to the King

HENRY, surnamed BOLING-BROKE, Duke of Hereford, son of John of Gaunt, afterwards King Henry IV

DUKE OF AUMERLE, son of the Duke of York

THOMAS MOWBRAY, Duke of Norfolk

DUKE OF SURREY

EARL OF SALISBURY

EARL BERKELEY

BUSHY- favourites of King Richard

BAGOT -   "   "   "   "

GREEN -   "   "   "   "

EARL OF NORTHUMBER-LAND

HENRY PERCY, surnamed HOT-SPUR, his son

LORD ROSS

LORD WILLOUGHBY

LORD FITZWATER

BISHOP OF CARLISLE

ABBOT OF WESTMINSTER

LORD MARSHAL

SIR STEPHEN SCROOP

SIR PIERCE OF EXTON

CAPTAIN of a band of Welshmen

TWO GARDENERS

QUEEN to King Richard

DUCHESS OF YORK

DUCHESS OF GLOUCESTER, widow of Thomas of Woodstock,

DUKE OF GLOUCESTER

LADY attending on the Queen

Lords, Heralds, Officers, Soldiers, Keeper, Messenger, Groom, and other Attendants

SCENE: England and Wales

ACT I

SCENE I

London. The palace

Enter RICHARD, JOHN OF GAUNT, with other
NOBLES and attendants

KING RICHARD. Old John of Gaunt, time-honoured
Lancaster,
Hast thou, according to thy oath and band,
Brought hither Henry Hereford, thy bold son,
Here to make good the boist'rous late appeal,
Which then our leisure would not let us hear,
Against the Duke of Norfolk, Thomas Mowbray?

GAUNT. I have, my liege.

KING RICHARD. Tell me, moreover, hast thou
sounded him
If he appeal the Duke on ancient malice,
Or worthily, as a good subject should,
On some known ground of treachery in him?

GAUNT. As near as I could sift him on that argument,
On some apparent danger seen in him
Aim'd at your Highness-no inveterate malice.

KING RICHARD. Then call them to our presence: face
to face
And frowning brow to brow, ourselves will hear
The accuser and the accused freely speak.
High-stomach'd are they both and full of ire,
In rage, deaf as the sea, hasty as fire.

Enter BOLINGBROKE and MOWBRAY

BOLINGBROKE. Many years of happy days befall
My gracious sovereign, my most loving liege!

MOWBRAY. Each day still better other's happiness
Until the heavens, envying earth's good hap,
Add an immortal title to your crown!

KING RICHARD. We thank you both; yet one but
flatters us,
As well appeareth by the cause you come;
Namely, to appeal each other of high treason.
Cousin of Hereford, what dost thou object
Against the Duke of Norfolk, Thomas Mowbray?

BOLINGBROKE. First-heaven be the record to my
speech!
In the devotion of a subject's love,
Tend'ring the precious safety of my prince,
And free from other misbegotten hate,
Come I appellant to this princely presence.
Now, Thomas Mowbray, do I turn to thee,
And mark my greeting well; for what I speak
My body shall make good upon this earth,
Or my divine soul answer it in heaven-
Thou art a traitor and a miscreant,
Too good to be so, and too bad to live,
Since the more fair and crystal is the sky,
The uglier seem the clouds that in it fly.
Once more, the more to aggravate the note,
With a foul traitor's name stuff I thy throat;
And wish-so please my sovereign-ere I move,
What my tongue speaks, my right drawn sword may
prove.

MOWBRAY. Let not my cold words here accuse my
zeal.
'Tis not the trial of a woman's war,
The bitter clamour of two eager tongues,
Can arbitrate this cause betwixt us twain;
The blood is hot that must be cool'd for this.
Yet can I not of such tame patience boast
As to be hush'd and nought at all to say.

First, the fair reverence of your Highness curbs me
From giving reins and spurs to my free speech;
Which else would post until it had return'd
These terms of treason doubled down his throat.
Setting aside his high blood's royalty,
And let him be no kinsman to my liege,
I do defy him, and I spit at him,
Call him a slanderous coward and a villain;
Which to maintain, I would allow him odds
And meet him, were I tied to run afoot
Even to the frozen ridges of the Alps,
Or any other ground inhabitable
Where ever Englishman durst set his foot.
Meantime let this defend my loyalty-
By all my hopes, most falsely doth he lie

BOLINGBROKE. Pale trembling coward, there I throw my gage,
Disclaiming here the kindred of the King;
And lay aside my high blood's royalty,
Which fear, not reverence, makes thee to except.
If guilty dread have left thee so much strength
As to take up mine honour's pawn, then stoop.
By that and all the rites of knighthood else
Will I make good against thee, arm to arm,
What I have spoke or thou canst worst devise.

MOWBRAY. I take it up; and by that sword I swear
Which gently laid my knighthood on my shoulder
I'll answer thee in any fair degree
Or chivalrous design of knightly trial;
And when I mount, alive may I not light
If I be traitor or unjustly fight!

KING RICHARD. What doth our cousin lay to Mowbray's charge?
It must be great that can inherit us
So much as of a thought of ill in him.

BOLINGBROKE. Look what I speak, my life shall

prove it true-
That Mowbray hath receiv'd eight thousand nobles
In name of lendings for your Highness' soldiers,
The which he hath detain'd for lewd employments
Like a false traitor and injurious villain.
Besides, I say and will in battle prove-
Or here, or elsewhere to the furthest verge
That ever was survey'd by English eye-
That all the treasons for these eighteen years
Complotted and contrived in this land
Fetch from false Mowbray their first head and spring.
Further I say, and further will maintain
Upon his bad life to make all this good,
That he did plot the Duke of Gloucester's death,
Suggest his soon-believing adversaries,
And consequently, like a traitor coward,
Sluic'd out his innocent soul through streams of blood;
Which blood, like sacrificing Abel's, cries,
Even from the tongueless caverns of the earth,
To me for justice and rough chastisement;
And, by the glorious worth of my descent,
This arm shall do it, or this life be spent.

KING RICHARD. How high a pitch his resolution
soars!
Thomas of Norfolk, what say'st thou to this?

MOWBRAY. O, let my sovereign turn away his face
And bid his ears a little while be deaf,
Till I have told this slander of his blood
How God and good men hate so foul a liar.

KING RICHARD. Mowbray, impartial are our eyes
and cars.
Were he my brother, nay, my kingdom's heir,
As he is but my father's brother's son,
Now by my sceptre's awe I make a vow,
Such neighbour nearness to our sacred blood
Should nothing privilege him nor partialize

The unstooping firmness of my upright soul.
He is our subject, Mowbray; so art thou:
Free speech and fearless I to thee allow.

MOWBRAY. Then, Bolingbroke, as low as to thy heart,
Through the false passage of thy throat, thou liest.
Three parts of that receipt I had for Calais
Disburs'd I duly to his Highness' soldiers;
The other part reserv'd I by consent,
For that my sovereign liege was in my debt
Upon remainder of a dear account
Since last I went to France to fetch his queen:
Now swallow down that lie. For Gloucester's death-
I slew him not, but to my own disgrace
Neglected my sworn duty in that case.
For you, my noble Lord of Lancaster,
The honourable father to my foe,
Once did I lay an ambush for your life,
A trespass that doth vex my grieved soul;
But ere I last receiv'd the sacrament
I did confess it, and exactly begg'd
Your Grace's pardon; and I hope I had it.
This is my fault. As for the rest appeal'd,
It issues from the rancour of a villain,
A recreant and most degenerate traitor;
Which in myself I boldly will defend,
And interchangeably hurl down my gage
Upon this overweening traitor's foot
To prove myself a loyal gentleman
Even in the best blood chamber'd in his bosom.
In haste whereof, most heartily I pray
Your Highness to assign our trial day.

KING RICHARD. Wrath-kindled gentlemen, be rul'd
by me;
Let's purge this choler without letting blood-
This we prescribe, though no physician;
Deep malice makes too deep incision.
Forget, forgive; conclude and be agreed:

Our doctors say this is no month to bleed.
Good uncle, let this end where it begun;
We'll calm the Duke of Norfolk, you your son.

GAUNT. To be a make-peace shall become my age.
Throw down, my son, the Duke of Norfolk's gage.

KING RICHARD. And, Norfolk, throw down his.

GAUNT. When, Harry, when?
Obedience bids I should not bid again.

KING RICHARD. Norfolk, throw down; we bid.
There is no boot.

MOWBRAY. Myself I throw, dread sovereign, at thy
foot;
My life thou shalt command, but not my shame:
The one my duty owes; but my fair name,
Despite of death, that lives upon my grave
To dark dishonour's use thou shalt not have.
I am disgrac'd, impeach'd, and baffl'd here;
Pierc'd to the soul with slander's venom'd spear,
The which no balm can cure but his heart-blood
Which breath'd this poison.

KING RICHARD. Rage must be withstood:
Give me his gage-lions make leopards tame.

MOWBRAY. Yea, but not change his spots. Take but
my shame,
And I resign my gage. My dear dear lord,
The purest treasure mortal times afford
Is spotless reputation; that away,
Men are but gilded loam or painted clay.
A jewel in a ten-times barr'd-up chest
Is a bold spirit in a loyal breast.
Mine honour is my life; both grow in one;
Take honour from me, and my life is done:
Then, dear my liege, mine honour let me try;
In that I live, and for that will I die.

KING RICHARD. Cousin, throw up your gage; do you begin.

BOLINGBROKE. O, God defend my soul from such deep sin!
Shall I seem crest-fallen in my father's sight?
Or with pale beggar-fear impeach my height
Before this outdar'd dastard? Ere my tongue
Shall wound my honour with such feeble wrong
Or sound so base a parle, my teeth shall tear
The slavish motive of recanting fear,
And spit it bleeding in his high disgrace,
Where shame doth harbour, even in Mowbray's face.

Exit GAUNT

KING RICHARD. We were not born to sue, but to command;
Which since we cannot do to make you friends,
Be ready, as your lives shall answer it,
At Coventry, upon Saint Lambert's day.
There shall your swords and lances arbitrate
The swelling difference of your settled hate;
Since we can not atone you, we shall see
Justice design the victor's chivalry.
Lord Marshal, command our officers-at-arms
Be ready to direct these home alarms.   *Exeunt*

SCENE II

London. The DUKE OF LANCASTER'S palace

Enter JOHN OF GAUNT with the DUCHESS OF GLOUCESTER

GAUNT. Alas, the part I had in Woodstock's blood
Doth more solicit me than your exclaims
To stir against the butchers of his life!
But since correction lieth in those hands

Which made the fault that we cannot correct,
Put we our quarrel to the will of heaven;
Who, when they see the hours ripe on earth,
Will rain hot vengeance on offenders' heads.

DUCHESS. Finds brotherhood in thee no sharper spur?
Hath love in thy old blood no living fire?
Edward's seven sons, whereof thyself art one,
Were as seven vials of his sacred blood,
Or seven fair branches springing from one root.
Some of those seven are dried by nature's course,
Some of those branches by the Destinies cut;
But Thomas, my dear lord, my life, my Gloucester,
One vial full of Edward's sacred blood,
One flourishing branch of his most royal root,
Is crack'd, and all the precious liquor spilt;
Is hack'd down, and his summer leaves all faded,
By envy's hand and murder's bloody axe.
Ah, Gaunt, his blood was thine! That bed, that womb,
That mettle, that self mould, that fashion'd thee,
Made him a man; and though thou livest and breathest,
Yet art thou slain in him. Thou dost consent
In some large measure to thy father's death
In that thou seest thy wretched brother die,
Who was the model of thy father's life.
Call it not patience, Gaunt-it is despair;
In suff'ring thus thy brother to be slaught'red,
Thou showest the naked pathway to thy life,
Teaching stern murder how to butcher thee.
That which in mean men we entitle patience
Is pale cold cowardice in noble breasts.
What shall I say? To safeguard thine own life
The best way is to venge my Gloucester's death.

GAUNT. God's is the quarrel; for God's substitute,
His deputy anointed in His sight,
Hath caus'd his death; the which if wrongfully,
Let heaven revenge; for I may never lift
An angry arm against His minister.

DUCHESS. Where then, alas, may I complain myself?

GAUNT. To God, the widow's champion and defence.

DUCHESS. Why then, I will. Farewell, old Gaunt.
Thou goest to Coventry, there to behold
Our cousin Hereford and fell Mowbray fight.
O, sit my husband's wrongs on Hereford's spear,
That it may enter butcher Mowbray's breast!
Or, if misfortune miss the first career,
Be Mowbray's sins so heavy in his bosom
That they may break his foaming courser's back
And throw the rider headlong in the lists,
A caitiff recreant to my cousin Hereford!
Farewell, old Gaunt; thy sometimes brother's wife,
With her companion, Grief, must end her life.

GAUNT. Sister, farewell; I must to Coventry.
As much good stay with thee as go with me!

DUCHESS. Yet one word more- grief boundeth where it falls,
Not with the empty hollowness, but weight.
I take my leave before I have begun,
For sorrow ends not when it seemeth done.
Commend me to thy brother, Edmund York.
Lo, this is all- nay, yet depart not so;
Though this be all, do not so quickly go;
I shall remember more. Bid him- ah, what?-
With all good speed at Plashy visit me.
Alack, and what shall good old York there see
But empty lodgings and unfurnish'd walls,
Unpeopled offices, untrodden stones?
And what hear there for welcome but my groans?
Therefore commend me; let him not come there
To seek out sorrow that dwells every where.
Desolate, desolate, will I hence and die;
The last leave of thee takes my weeping eye.   *Exeunt*

SCENE III

The lists at Coventry

*Enter the LORD MARSHAL and the DUKE OF
AUMERLE*

MARSHAL. My Lord Aumerle, is Harry Hereford
arm'd?

AUMERLE. Yea, at all points; and longs to enter in.

MARSHAL. The Duke of Norfolk, spightfully and
bold,
Stays but the summons of the appelant's trumpet.

AUMERLE. Why then, the champions are prepar'd,
and stay
For nothing but his Majesty's approach.

*The trumpets sound, and the KING enters with his nobles,
GAUNT, BUSHY, BAGOT, GREEN, and others. When
they are set, enter MOWBRAY, Duke of Nor folk, in arms,
defendant, and a HERALD*

KING RICHARD. Marshal, demand of yonder cham-
pion
The cause of his arrival here in arms;
Ask him his name; and orderly proceed
To swear him in the justice of his cause.

MARSHAL. In God's name and the King's, say who
thou art,
And why thou comest thus knightly clad in arms;
Against what man thou com'st, and what thy quarrel.
Speak truly on thy knighthood and thy oath;
As so defend thee heaven and thy valour!

MOWBRAY. My name is Thomas Mowbray, Duke of
Norfolk;
Who hither come engaged by my oath-

Which God defend a knight should violate!-
Both to defend my loyalty and truth
To God, my King, and my succeeding issue,
Against the Duke of Hereford that appeals me;
And, by the grace of God and this mine arm,
To prove him, in defending of myself,
A traitor to my God, my King, and me.
And as I truly fight, defend me heaven!

The trumpets sound. Enter BOLINGBROKE, Duke of Hereford, appellant, in armour, and a HERALD

KING RICHARD. Marshal, ask yonder knight in arms,
Both who he is and why he cometh hither
Thus plated in habiliments of war;
And formally, according to our law,
Depose him in the justice of his cause.

MARSHAL. What is thy name? and wherefore com'st thou hither
Before King Richard in his royal lists?
Against whom comest thou? and what's thy quarrel?
Speak like a true knight, so defend thee heaven!

BOLINGBROKE. Harry of Hereford, Lancaster, and Derby,
Am I; who ready here do stand in arms
To prove, by God's grace and my body's valour,
In lists on Thomas Mowbray, Duke of Norfolk,
That he is a traitor, foul and dangerous,
To God of heaven, King Richard, and to me.
And as I truly fight, defend me heaven!

MARSHAL. On pain of death, no person be so bold
Or daring-hardy as to touch the lists,
Except the Marshal and such officers
Appointed to direct these fair designs.

BOLINGBROKE. Lord Marshal, let me kiss my sovereign's hand,

And bow my knee before his Majesty;
For Mowbray and myself are like two men
That vow a long and weary pilgrimage.
Then let us take a ceremonious leave
And loving farewell of our several friends.

MARSHAL. The appellant in all duty greets your
Highness,
And craves to kiss your hand and take his leave.

KING RICHARD. We will descend and fold him in
our arms.
Cousin of Hereford, as thy cause is right,
So be thy fortune in this royal fight!
Farewell, my blood; which if to-day thou shed,
Lament we may, but not revenge thee dead.

BOLINGBROKE. O, let no noble eye profane a tear
For me, if I be gor'd with Mowbray's spear.
As confident as is the falcon's flight
Against a bird, do I with Mowbray fight.
My loving lord, I take my leave of you;
Of you, my noble cousin, Lord Aumerle;
Not sick, although I have to do with death,
But lusty, young, and cheerly drawing breath.
Lo, as at English feasts, so I regreet
The daintiest last, to make the end most sweet.
O thou, the earthly author of my blood,
Whose youthful spirit, in me regenerate,
Doth with a twofold vigour lift me up
To reach at victory above my head,
Add proof unto mine armour with thy prayers,
And with thy blessings steel my lance's point,
That it may enter Mowbray's waxen coat
And furbish new the name of John o' Gaunt,
Even in the lusty haviour of his son.

GAUNT. God in thy good cause make thee prosperous!
Be swift like lightning in the execution,
And let thy blows, doubly redoubled,

Fall like amazing thunder on the casque
Of thy adverse pernicious enemy.
Rouse up thy youthful blood, be valiant, and live.

BOLINGBROKE. Mine innocence and Saint George to
thrive!

MOWBRAY. However God or fortune cast my lot,
There lives or dies, true to King Richard's throne,
A loyal, just, and upright gentleman.
Never did captive with a freer heart
Cast off his chains of bondage, and embrace
His golden uncontroll'd enfranchisement,
More than my dancing soul doth celebrate
This feast of battle with mine adversary.
Most mighty liege, and my companion peers,
Take from my mouth the wish of happy years.
As gentle and as jocund as to jest
Go I to fight: truth hath a quiet breast.

KING RICHARD. Farewell, my lord, securely I espy
Virtue with valour couched in thine eye.
Order the trial, Marshal, and begin.

MARSHAL. Harry of Hereford, Lancaster, and Derby,
Receive thy lance; and God defend the right!

BOLINGBROKE. Strong as a tower in hope, I cry amen.

MARSHAL. *[To an OFFICER]* Go bear this lance to
Thomas,
Duke of Norfolk.

FIRST HERALD. Harry of Hereford, Lancaster, and
Derby,
Stands here for God, his sovereign, and himself,
On pain to be found false and recreant,
To prove the Duke of Norfolk, Thomas Mowbray,
A traitor to his God, his King, and him;
And dares him to set forward to the fight.

SECOND HERALD. Here standeth Thomas Mowbray,

Duke of Norfolk,
On pain to be found false and recreant,
Both to defend himself, and to approve
Henry of Hereford, Lancaster, and Derby,
To God, his sovereign, and to him disloyal,
Courageously and with a free desire
Attending but the signal to begin.

MARSHAL. Sound trumpets; and set forward, combat-
ants. *[A charge sounded]*
Stay, the King hath thrown his warder down.

KING RICHARD. Let them lay by their helmets and
their spears,
And both return back to their chairs again.
Withdraw with us; and let the trumpets sound
While we return these dukes what we decree.

[A long flourish, while the KING consults his Council]

Draw near,
And list what with our council we have done.
For that our kingdom's earth should not be soil'd
With that dear blood which it hath fostered;
And for our eyes do hate the dire aspect
Of civil wounds plough'd up with neighbours' sword;
And for we think the eagle-winged pride
Of sky-aspiring and ambitious thoughts,
With rival-hating envy, set on you
To wake our peace, which in our country's cradle
Draws the sweet infant breath of gentle sleep;
Which so rous'd up with boist'rous untun'd drums,
With harsh-resounding trumpets' dreadful bray,
And grating shock of wrathful iron arms,
Might from our quiet confines fright fair peace
And make us wade even in our kindred's blood-
Therefore we banish you our territories.
You, cousin Hereford, upon pain of life,
Till twice five summers have enrich'd our fields
Shall not regreet our fair dominions,

But tread the stranger paths of banishment.

BOLINGBROKE. Your will be done. This must my comfort be-
That sun that warms you here shall shine on me,
And those his golden beams to you here lent
Shall point on me and gild my banishment.

KING RICHARD. Norfolk, for thee remains a heavier doom,
Which I with some unwillingness pronounce:
The sly slow hours shall not determinate
The dateless limit of thy dear exile;
The hopeless word of 'never to return'
Breathe I against thee, upon pain of life.

MOWBRAY. A heavy sentence, my most sovereign liege,
And all unlook'd for from your Highness' mouth.
A dearer merit, not so deep a maim
As to be cast forth in the common air,
Have I deserved at your Highness' hands.
The language I have learnt these forty years,
My native English, now I must forgo;
And now my tongue's use is to me no more
Than an unstringed viol or a harp;
Or like a cunning instrument cas'd up
Or, being open, put into his hands
That knows no touch to tune the harmony.
Within my mouth you have engaol'd my tongue,
Doubly portcullis'd with my teeth and lips;
And dull, unfeeling, barren ignorance
Is made my gaoler to attend on me.
I am too old to fawn upon a nurse,
Too far in years to be a pupil now.
What is thy sentence, then, but speechless death,
Which robs my tongue from breathing native breath?

KING RICHARD. It boots thee not to be compassionate;

After our sentence plaining comes too late.

MOWBRAY. Then thus I turn me from my countrv's light,
To dwell in solemn shades of endless night.

KING RICHARD. Return again, and take an oath with thee.
Lay on our royal sword your banish'd hands;
Swear by the duty that you owe to God,
Our part therein we banish with yourselves,
To keep the oath that we administer:
You never shall, so help you truth and God,
Embrace each other's love in banishment;
Nor never look upon each other's face;
Nor never write, regreet, nor reconcile
This louring tempest of your home-bred hate;
Nor never by advised purpose meet
To plot, contrive, or complot any ill,
'Gainst us, our state, our subjects, or our land.

BOLINGBROKE. I swear.

MOWBRAY. And I, to keep all this.

BOLINGBROKE. Norfolk, so far as to mine enemy.
By this time, had the King permitted us,
One of our souls had wand'red in the air,
Banish'd this frail sepulchre of our flesh,
As now our flesh is banish'd from this land-
Confess thy treasons ere thou fly the realm;
Since thou hast far to go, bear not along
The clogging burden of a guilty soul.

MOWBRAY. No, Bolingbroke; if ever I were traitor,
My name be blotted from the book of life,
And I from heaven banish'd as from hence!
But what thou art, God, thou, and I, do know;
And all too soon, I fear, the King shall rue.
Farewell, my liege. Now no way can I stray:
Save back to England, an the world's my way.   *Exit*

KING RICHARD. Uncle, even in the glasses of thine eyes
I see thy grieved heart. Thy sad aspect
Hath from the number of his banish'd years
Pluck'd four away. *[To BOLINGBROKE]* Six frozen winters spent,
Return with welcome home from banishment.

BOLINGBROKE. How long a time lies in one little word!
Four lagging winters and four wanton springs
End in a word: such is the breath of Kings.

GAUNT. I thank my liege that in regard of me
He shortens four years of my son's exile;
But little vantage shall I reap thereby,
For ere the six years that he hath to spend
Can change their moons and bring their times about,
My oil-dried lamp and time-bewasted light
Shall be extinct with age and endless night;
My inch of taper will be burnt and done,
And blindfold death not let me see my son.

KING RICHARD. Why, uncle, thou hast many years to live.

GAUNT. But not a minute, King, that thou canst give:
Shorten my days thou canst with sullen sorrow
And pluck nights from me, but not lend a morrow;
Thou can'st help time to furrow me with age,
But stop no wrinkle in his pilgrimage;
Thy word is current with him for my death,
But dead, thy kingdom cannot buy my breath.

KING RICHARD. Thy son is banish'd upon good advice,
Whereto thy tongue a party-verdict gave.
Why at our justice seem'st thou then to lour?

GAUNT. Things sweet to taste prove in digestion sour.
You urg'd me as a judge; but I had rather

William Shakespeare

You would have bid me argue like a father.
O, had it been a stranger, not my child,
To smooth his fault I should have been more mild.
A partial slander sought I to avoid,
And in the sentence my own life destroy'd.
Alas, I look'd when some of you should say
I was too strict to make mine own away;
But you gave leave to my unwilling tongue
Against my will to do myself this wrong.

KING RICHARD. Cousin, farewell; and, uncle, bid him so.
Six years we banish him, and he shall go.

> *Flourish. Exit KING with train*

AUMERLE. Cousin, farewell; what presence must not know,
From where you do remain let paper show.

MARSHAL. My lord, no leave take I, for I will ride
As far as land will let me by your side.

GAUNT. O, to what purpose dost thou hoard thy words,
That thou returnest no greeting to thy friends?

BOLINGBROKE. I have too few to take my leave of you,
When the tongue's office should be prodigal
To breathe the abundant dolour of the heart.

GAUNT. Thy grief is but thy absence for a time.

BOLINGBROKE. Joy absent, grief is present for that time.

GAUNT. What is six winters? They are quickly gone.

BOLINGBROKE. To men in joy; but grief makes one hour ten.

GAUNT. Call it a travel that thou tak'st for pleasure.

BOLINGBROKE. My heart will sigh when I miscall

it so,
Which finds it an enforced pilgrimage.

GAUNT. The sullen passage of thy weary steps
Esteem as foil wherein thou art to set
The precious jewel of thy home return.

BOLINGBROKE. Nay, rather, every tedious stride I
make
Will but remember me what a deal of world
I wander from the jewels that I love.
Must I not serve a long apprenticehood
To foreign passages; and in the end,
Having my freedom, boast of nothing else
But that I was a journeyman to grief?

GAUNT. All places that the eye of heaven visits
Are to a wise man ports and happy havens.
Teach thy necessity to reason thus:
There is no virtue like necessity.
Think not the King did banish thee,
But thou the King. Woe doth the heavier sit
Where it perceives it is but faintly home.
Go, say I sent thee forth to purchase honour,
And not the King exil'd thee; or suppose
Devouring pestilence hangs in our air
And thou art flying to a fresher clime.
Look what thy soul holds dear, imagine it
To lie that way thou goest, not whence thou com'st.
Suppose the singing birds musicians,
The grass whereon thou tread'st the presence strew'd,
The flowers fair ladies, and thy steps no more
Than a delightful measure or a dance;
For gnarling sorrow hath less power to bite
The man that mocks at it and sets it light.

BOLINGBROKE. O, who can hold a fire in his hand
By thinking on the frosty Caucasus?
Or cloy the hungry edge of appetite
By bare imagination of a feast?

Or wallow naked in December snow
By thinking on fantastic summer's heat?
O, no! the apprehension of the good
Gives but the greater feeling to the worse.
Fell sorrow's tooth doth never rankle more
Than when he bites, but lanceth not the sore.

GAUNT. Come, come, my son, I'll bring thee on thy
way.
Had I thy youtli and cause, I would not stay.

BOLINGBROKE. Then, England's ground, farewell;
sweet soil, adieu;
My mother, and my nurse, that bears me yet!
Where'er I wander, boast of this I can:
Though banish'd, yet a trueborn English man.   *Exeunt*

SCENE IV

London. The court

*Enter the KING, with BAGOT and GREEN, at one door;
and the DUKE OF AUMERLE at another*

KING RICHARD. We did observe. Cousin Aumerle,
How far brought you high Hereford on his way?

AUMERLE. I brought high Hereford, if you call him
so,
But to the next high way, and there I left him.

KING RICHARD. And say, what store of parting tears
were shed?

AUMERLE. Faith, none for me; except the north-east
wind,
Which then blew bitterly against our faces,
Awak'd the sleeping rheum, and so by chance
Did grace our hollow parting with a tear.

KING RICHARD. What said our cousin when you parted with him?

AUMERLE. 'Farewell.'
And, for my heart disdained that my tongue
Should so profane the word, that taught me craft
To counterfeit oppression of such grief
That words seem'd buried in my sorrow's grave.
Marry, would the word 'farewell' have length'ned hours
And added years to his short banishment,
He should have had a volume of farewells;
But since it would not, he had none of me.

KING RICHARD. He is our cousin, cousin; but 'tis doubt,
When time shall call him home from banishment,
Whether our kinsman come to see his friends.
Ourself, and Bushy, Bagot here, and Green,
Observ'd his courtship to the common people;
How he did seem to dive into their hearts
With humble and familiar courtesy;
What reverence he did throw away on slaves,
Wooing poor craftsmen with the craft of smiles
And patient underbearing of his fortune,
As 'twere to banish their affects with him.
Off goes his bonnet to an oyster-wench;
A brace of draymen bid God speed him well
And had the tribute of his supple knee,
With 'Thanks, my countrymen, my loving friends';
As were our England in reversion his,
And he our subjects' next degree in hope.

GREEN. Well, he is gone; and with him go these thoughts!
Now for the rebels which stand out in Ireland,
Expedient manage must be made, my liege,
Ere further leisure yicld them further means
For their advantage and your Highness' loss.

KING RICHARD. We will ourself in person to this war;

And, for our coffers, with too great a court
And liberal largess, are grown somewhat light,
We are enforc'd to farm our royal realm;
The revenue whereof shall furnish us
For our affairs in hand. If that come short,
Our substitutes at home shall have blank charters;
Whereto, when they shall know what men are rich,
They shall subscribe them for large sums of gold,
And send them after to supply our wants;
For we will make for Ireland presently.

Enter BUSHY

Bushy, what news?

BUSHY. Old John of Gaunt is grievous sick, my lord,
Suddenly taken; and hath sent poste-haste
To entreat your Majesty to visit him.

KING RICHARD. Where lies he?

BUSHY. At Ely House.

KING RICHARD. Now put it, God, in the physician's
mind
To help him to his grave immediately!
The lining of his coffers shall make coats
To deck our soldiers for these Irish wars.
Come, gentlemen, let's all go visit him.
Pray God we may make haste, and come too late!

ALL. Amen.   *Exeunt*

ACT II

SCENE I

London. Ely House

Enter JOHN OF GAUNT, sick, with the DUKE OF YORK, etc

GAUNT. Will the King come, that I may breathe my last
In wholesome counsel to his unstaid youth?

YORK. Vex not yourself, nor strive not with your breath;
For all in vain comes counsel to his ear.

GAUNT. O, but they say the tongues of dying men
Enforce attention like deep harmony.
Where words are scarce, they are seldom spent in vain;
For they breathe truth that breathe their words -in pain.
He that no more must say is listen'd more
Than they whom youth and ease have taught to glose;
More are men's ends mark'd than their lives before.
The setting sun, and music at the close,
As the last taste of sweets, is sweetest last,
Writ in remembrance more than things long past.
Though Richard my life's counsel would not hear,
My death's sad tale may yet undeaf his ear.

YORK. No; it is stopp'd with other flattering sounds,
As praises, of whose taste the wise are fond,
Lascivious metres, to whose venom sound
The open ear of youth doth always listen;
Report of fashions in proud Italy,
Whose manners still our tardy apish nation
Limps after in base imitation.
Where doth the world thrust forth a vanity-
So it be new, there's no respect how vile-
That is not quickly buzz'd into his ears?

Then all too late comes counsel to be heard
Where will doth mutiny with wit's regard.
Direct not him whose way himself will choose.
'Tis breath thou lack'st, and that breath wilt thou lose.

GAUNT. Methinks I am a prophet new inspir'd,
And thus expiring do foretell of him:
His rash fierce blaze of riot cannot last,
For violent fires soon burn out themselves;
Small showers last long, but sudden storms are short;
He tires betimes that spurs too fast betimes;
With eager feeding food doth choke the feeder;
Light vanity, insatiate cormorant,
Consuming means, soon preys upon itself.
This royal throne of kings, this scept'red isle,
This earth of majesty, this seat of Mars,
This other Eden, demi-paradise,
This fortress built by Nature for herself
Against infection and the hand of war,
This happy breed of men, this little world,
This precious stone set in the silver sea,
Which serves it in the office of a wall,
Or as a moat defensive to a house,
Against the envy of less happier lands;
This blessed plot, this earth, this realm, this England,
This nurse, this teeming womb of royal kings,
Fear'd by their breed, and famous by their birth,
Renowned for their deeds as far from home,
For Christian service and true chivalry,
As is the sepulchre in stubborn Jewry
Of the world's ransom, blessed Mary's Son;
This land of such dear souls, this dear dear land,
Dear for her reputation through the world,
Is now leas'd out-I die pronouncing it-
Like to a tenement or pelting farm.
England, bound in with the triumphant sea,
Whose rocky shore beats back the envious siege
Of wat'ry Neptune, is now bound in with shame,

With inky blots and rotten parchment bonds;
That England, that was wont to conquer others,
Hath made a shameful conquest of itself.
Ah, would the scandal vanish with my life,
How happy then were my ensuing death!

Enter KING and QUEEN, AUMERLE, BUSHY,
GREEN, BAGOT, ROSS, and WILLOUGHBY

YORK. The King is come; deal mildly with his youth,
For young hot colts being rag'd do rage the more.

QUEEN. How fares our noble uncle Lancaster?

KING RICHARD. What comfort, man? How is't with
aged Gaunt?

GAUNT. O, how that name befits my composition!
Old Gaunt, indeed; and gaunt in being old.
Within me grief hath kept a tedious fast;
And who abstains from meat that is not gaunt?
For sleeping England long time have I watch'd;
Watching breeds leanness, leanness is an gaunt.
The pleasure that some fathers feed upon
Is my strict fast-I mean my children's looks;
And therein fasting, hast thou made me gaunt.
Gaunt am I for the grave, gaunt as a grave,
Whose hollow womb inherits nought but bones.

KING RICHARD. Can sick men play so nicely with
their names?

GAUNT. No, misery makes sport to mock itself:
Since thou dost seek to kill my name in me,
I mock my name, great king, to flatter thee.

KING RICHARD. Should dying men flatter with those
that live?

GAUNT. No, no; men living flatter those that die.

KING RICHARD. Thou, now a-dying, sayest thou

flatterest me.

GAUNT. O, no! thou diest, though I the sicker be.

KING RICHARD. I am in health, I breathe, and see thee
ill.

GAUNT. Now He that made me knows I see thee ill;
Ill in myself to see, and in thee seeing ill.
Thy death-bed is no lesser than thy land
Wherein thou liest in reputation sick;
And thou, too careless patient as thou art,
Commit'st thy anointed body to the cure
Of those physicians that first wounded thee:
A thousand flatterers sit within thy crown,
Whose compass is no bigger than thy head;
And yet, incaged in so small a verge,
The waste is no whit lesser than thy land.
O, had thy grandsire with a prophet's eye
Seen how his son's son should destroy his sons,
From forth thy reach he would have laid thy shame,
Deposing thee before thou wert possess'd,
Which art possess'd now to depose thyself.
Why, cousin, wert thou regent of the world,
It were a shame to let this land by lease;
But for thy world enjoying but this land,
Is it not more than shame to shame it so?
Landlord of England art thou now, not King.
Thy state of law is bondslave to the law;
And thou-

KING RICHARD. A lunatic lean-witted fool,
Presuming on an ague's privilege,
Darest with thy frozen admonition
Make pale our cheek, chasing the royal blood
With fury from his native residence.
Now by my seat's right royal majesty,
Wert thou not brother to great Edward's son,
This tongue that runs so roundly in thy head
Should run thy head from thy unreverent shoulders.

GAUNT. O, Spare me not, my brother Edward's son,
For that I was his father Edward's son;
That blood already, like the pelican,
Hast thou tapp'd out, and drunkenly carous'd.
My brother Gloucester, plain well-meaning soul-
Whom fair befall in heaven 'mongst happy souls!-
May be a precedent and witness good
That thou respect'st not spilling Edward's blood.
Join with the present sickness that I have;
And thy unkindness be like crooked age,
To crop at once a too long withered flower.
Live in thy shame, but die not shame with thee!
These words hereafter thy tormentors be!
Convey me to my bed, then to my grave.
Love they to live that love and honour have.

Exit, borne out by his attendants

KING RICHARD. And let them die that age and sul-
lens have;
For both hast thou, and both become the grave.

YORK. I do beseech your Majesty impute his words
To wayward sickliness and age in him.
He loves you, on my life, and holds you dear
As Harry Duke of Hereford, were he here.

KING RICHARD. Right, you say true: as Hereford's
love, so his;
As theirs, so mine; and all be as it is.

Enter NORTHUMBERLAND

NORTHUMBERLAND. My liege, old Gaunt commends him to your Majesty.

KING RICHARD. What says he?

NORTHUMBERLAND. Nay, nothing; all is said.
His tongue is now a stringless instrument;
Words, life, and all, old Lancaster hath spent.

YORK. Be York the next that must be bankrupt so!
Though death be poor, it ends a mortal woe.

KING RICHARD. The ripest fruit first falls, and so
doth he;
His time is spent, our pilgrimage must be.
So much for that. Now for our Irish wars.
We must supplant those rough rug-headed kerns,
Which live like venom where no venom else
But only they have privilege to live.
And for these great affairs do ask some charge,
Towards our assistance we do seize to us
The plate, coin, revenues, and moveables,
Whereof our uncle Gaunt did stand possess'd.

YORK. How long shall I be patient? Ah, how long
Shall tender duty make me suffer wrong?
Not Gloucester's death, nor Hereford's banishment,
Nor Gaunt's rebukes, nor England's private wrongs,
Nor the prevention of poor Bolingbroke
About his marriage, nor my own disgrace,
Have ever made me sour my patient cheek
Or bend one wrinkle on my sovereign's face.
I am the last of noble Edward's sons,
Of whom thy father, Prince of Wales, was first.
In war was never lion rag'd more fierce,
In peace was never gentle lamb more mild,
Than was that young and princely gentleman.
His face thou hast, for even so look'd he,
Accomplish'd with the number of thy hours;
But when he frown'd, it was against the French
And not against his friends. His noble hand
Did win what he did spend, and spent not that
Which his triumphant father's hand had won.
His hands were guilty of no kindred blood,
But bloody with the enemies of his kin.
O Richard! York is too far gone with grief,
Or else he never would compare between-

KING RICHARD. Why, uncle, what's the matter?

YORK. O my liege,
Pardon me, if you please; if not, I, pleas'd
Not to be pardoned, am content withal.
Seek you to seize and gripe into your hands
The royalties and rights of banish'd Hereford?
Is not Gaunt dead? and doth not Hereford live?
Was not Gaunt just? and is not Harry true?
Did not the one deserve to have an heir?
Is not his heir a well-deserving son?
Take Hereford's rights away, and take from Time
His charters and his customary rights;
Let not to-morrow then ensue to-day;
Be not thyself-for how art thou a king
But by fair sequence and succession?
Now, afore God-God forbid I say true!-
If you do wrongfully seize Hereford's rights,
Call in the letters patents that he hath
By his attorneys-general to sue
His livery, and deny his off'red homage,
You pluck a thousand dangers on your head,
You lose a thousand well-disposed hearts,
And prick my tender patience to those thoughts
Which honour and allegiance cannot think.

KING RICHARD. Think what you will, we seize into
our hands
His plate, his goods, his money, and his lands.

YORK. I'll not be by the while. My liege, farewell.
What will ensue hereof there's none can tell;
But by bad courses may be understood
That their events can never fall out good.   *Exit*

KING RICHARD. Go, Bushy, to the Earl of Wiltshire
straight;
Bid him repair to us to Ely House
To see this business. To-morrow next
We will for Ireland; and 'tis time, I trow.

And we create, in absence of ourself,
Our Uncle York Lord Governor of England;
For he is just, and always lov'd us well.
Come on, our queen; to-morrow must we part;
Be merry, for our time of stay is short.

Flourish. Exeunt KING, QUEEN, BUSHY, AUMERLE,
GREEN, and BAGOT

NORTHUMBERLAND. Well, lords, the Duke of
Lancaster is dead.
Ross. And living too; for now his son is Duke.

WILLOUGHBY. Barely in title, not in revenues.

NORTHUMBERLAND. Richly in both, if justice had
her right.

ROSS. My heart is great; but it must break with silence,
Ere't be disburdened with a liberal tongue.

NORTHUMBERLAND. Nay, speak thy mind; and let
him ne'er speak more
That speaks thy words again to do thee harm!

WILLOUGHBY. Tends that thou wouldst speak to the
Duke of Hereford?
If it be so, out with it boldly, man;
Quick is mine ear to hear of good towards him.

ROSS. No good at all that I can do for him;
Unless you call it good to pity him,
Bereft and gelded of his patrimony.

NORTHUMBERLAND. Now, afore God, 'tis shame
such wrongs are borne
In him, a royal prince, and many moe
Of noble blood in this declining land.
The King is not himself, but basely led
By flatterers; and what they will inform,
Merely in hate, 'gainst any of us an,
That will the King severely prosecute
'Gainst us, our lives, our children, and our heirs.

ROSS. The commons hath he pill'd with grievous taxes;
And quite lost their hearts; the nobles hath he find
For ancient quarrels and quite lost their hearts.

WILLOUGHBY. And daily new exactions are devis'd,
As blanks, benevolences, and I wot not what;
But what, a God's name, doth become of this?

NORTHUMBERLAND. Wars hath not wasted it, for
warr'd he hath not,
But basely yielded upon compromise
That which his noble ancestors achiev'd with blows.
More hath he spent in peace than they in wars.

ROSS. The Earl of Wiltshire hath the realm in farm.

WILLOUGHBY. The King's grown bankrupt like a broken man.

NORTHUMBERLAND. Reproach and dissolution
hangeth over him.

ROSS. He hath not money for these Irish wars,
His burdenous taxations notwithstanding,
But by the robbing of the banish'd Duke.

NORTHUMBERLAND. His noble kinsman-most
degenerate king!
But, lords, we hear this fearful tempest sing,
Yet seek no shelter to avoid the storm;
We see the wind sit sore upon our sails,
And yet we strike not, but securely perish.

ROSS. We see the very wreck that we must suffer;
And unavoided is the danger now
For suffering so the causes of our wreck.

NORTHUMBERLAND. Not so; even through the hol-
low eyes of death
I spy life peering; but I dare not say
How near the tidings of our comfort is.

WILLOUGHBY. Nay, let us share thy thoughts as thou

dost ours.

ROSS. Be confident to speak, Northumberland.
We three are but thyself, and, speaking so,
Thy words are but as thoughts; therefore be bold.

NORTHUMBERLAND. Then thus: I have from Le
Port Blanc, a bay
In Brittany, receiv'd intelligence
That Harry Duke of Hereford, Rainold Lord Cobham,
That late broke from the Duke of Exeter,
His brother, Archbishop late of Canterbury,
Sir Thomas Erpingham, Sir John Ramston,
Sir John Norbery, Sir Robert Waterton, and Francis
Quoint-
All these, well furnish'd by the Duke of Britaine,
With eight tall ships, three thousand men of war,
Are making hither with all due expedience,
And shortly mean to touch our northern shore.
Perhaps they had ere this, but that they stay
The first departing of the King for Ireland.
If then we shall shake off our slavish yoke,
Imp out our drooping country's broken wing,
Redeem from broking pawn the blemish'd crown,
Wipe off the dust that hides our sceptre's gilt,
And make high majesty look like itself,
Away with me in post to Ravenspurgh;
But if you faint, as fearing to do so,
Stay and be secret, and myself will go.

ROSS. To horse, to horse! Urge doubts to them that fear.

WILLOUGHBY. Hold out my horse, and I will first be
there.   *Exeunt*

SCENE II

Windsor Castle

Enter QUEEN, BUSHY, and BAGOT

BUSHY. Madam, your Majesty is too much sad.
You promis'd, when you parted with the King,
To lay aside life-harming heaviness
And entertain a cheerful disposition.

QUEEN. To please the King, I did; to please myself
I cannot do it; yet I know no cause
Why I should welcome such a guest as grief,
Save bidding farewell to so sweet a guest
As my sweet Richard. Yet again methinks
Some unborn sorrow, ripe in fortune's womb,
Is coming towards me, and my inward soul
With nothing trembles. At some thing it grieves
More than with parting from my lord the King.

BUSHY. Each substance of a grief hath twenty shadows,
Which shows like grief itself, but is not so;
For sorrow's eye, glazed with blinding tears,
Divides one thing entire to many objects,
Like perspectives which, rightly gaz'd upon,
Show nothing but confusion-ey'd awry,
Distinguish form. So your sweet Majesty,
Looking awry upon your lord's departure,
Find shapes of grief more than himself to wail;
Which, look'd on as it is, is nought but shadows
Of what it is not. Then, thrice-gracious Queen,
More than your lord's departure weep not-more is not seen;
Or if it be, 'tis with false sorrow's eye,
Which for things true weeps things imaginary.

QUEEN. It may be so; but yet my inward soul
Persuades me it is otherwise. Howe'er it be,

I cannot but be sad; so heavy sad
As-though, on thinking, on no thought I think-
Makes me with heavy nothing faint and shrink.

BUSHY. 'Tis nothing but conceit, my gracious lady.

QUEEN. 'Tis nothing less: conceit is still deriv'd
From some forefather grief; mine is not so,
For nothing hath begot my something grief,
Or something hath the nothing that I grieve;
'Tis in reversion that I do possess-
But what it is that is not yet known what,
I cannot name; 'tis nameless woe, I wot.

Enter GREEN

GREEN. God save your Majesty! and well met, gentlemen.
I hope the King is not yet shipp'd for Ireland.

QUEEN. Why hopest thou so? 'Tis better hope he is;
For his designs crave haste, his haste good hope.
Then wherefore dost thou hope he is not shipp'd?

GREEN. That he, our hope, might have retir'd his
power
And driven into despair an enemy's hope
Who strongly hath set footing in this land.
The banish'd Bolingbroke repeals himself,
And with uplifted arms is safe arriv'd
At Ravenspurgh.

QUEEN. Now God in heaven forbid!

GREEN. Ah, madam, 'tis too true; and that is worse,
The Lord Northumberland, his son young Henry Percy,
The Lords of Ross, Beaumond, and Willoughby,
With all their powerful friends, are fled to him.

BUSHY. Why have you not proclaim'd Northumberland
And all the rest revolted faction traitors?

GREEN. We have; whereupon the Earl of Worcester
Hath broken his staff, resign'd his stewardship,
And all the household servants fled with him
To Bolingbroke.

QUEEN. So, Green, thou art the midwife to my woe,
And Bolingbroke my sorrow's dismal heir.
Now hath my soul brought forth her prodigy;
And I, a gasping new-deliver'd mother,
Have woe to woe, sorrow to sorrow join'd.

BUSHY. Despair not, madam.

QUEEN. Who shall hinder me?
I will despair, and be at enmity
With cozening hope-he is a flatterer,
A parasite, a keeper-back of death,
Who gently would dissolve the bands of life,
Which false hope lingers in extremity.

Enter YORK

GREEN. Here comes the Duke of York.

QUEEN. With signs of war about his aged neck.
O, full of careful business are his looks!
Uncle, for God's sake, speak comfortable words.

YORK. Should I do so, I should belie my thoughts.
Comfort's in heaven; and we are on the earth,
Where nothing lives but crosses, cares, and grief.
Your husband, he is gone to save far off,
Whilst others come to make him lose at home.
Here am I left to underprop his land,
Who, weak with age, cannot support myself.
Now comes the sick hour that his surfeit made;
Now shall he try his friends that flatter'd him.

Enter a SERVINGMAN

SERVINGMAN. My lord, your son was gone before

I came.

YORK. He was-why so go all which way it will!
The nobles they are fled, the commons they are cold
And will, I fear, revolt on Hereford's side.
Sirrah, get thee to Plashy, to my sister Gloucester;
Bid her send me presently a thousand pound.
Hold, take my ring.

SERVINGMAN. My lord, I had forgot to tell your
lordship,
To-day, as I came by, I called there-
But I shall grieve you to report the rest.

YORK. What is't, knave?

SERVINGMAN. An hour before I came, the Duchess
died.

YORK. God for his mercy! what a tide of woes
Comes rushing on this woeful land at once!
I know not what to do. I would to God,
So my untruth had not provok'd him to it,
The King had cut off my head with my brother's.
What, are there no posts dispatch'd for Ireland?
How shall we do for money for these wars?
Come, sister-cousin, I would say-pray, pardon me.
Go, fellow, get thee home, provide some carts,
And bring away the armour that is there.
                              Exit SERVINGMAN

Gentlemen, will you go muster men?
If I know how or which way to order these affairs
Thus disorderly thrust into my hands,
Never believe me. Both are my kinsmen.
T'one is my sovereign, whom both my oath
And duty bids defend; t'other again
Is my kinsman, whom the King hath wrong'd,
Whom conscience and my kindred bids to right.
Well, somewhat we must do.-Come, cousin,
I'll dispose of you. Gentlemen, go muster up your men

And meet me presently at Berkeley.
I should to Plashy too,
But time will not permit. All is uneven,
And everything is left at six and seven.

Exeunt YORK and QUEEN

BUSHY. The wind sits fair for news to go to Ireland.
But none returns. For us to levy power
Proportionable to the enemy
Is all unpossible.

GREEN. Besides, our nearness to the King in love
Is near the hate of those love not the King.

BAGOT. And that is the wavering commons; for their love
Lies in their purses; and whoso empties them,
By so much fills their hearts with deadly hate.

BUSHY. Wherein the King stands generally condemn'd.

BAGOT. If judgment lie in them, then so do we,
Because we ever have been near the King.

GREEN. Well, I will for refuge straight to Bristow Castle.
The Earl of Wiltshire is already there.

BUSHY. Thither will I with you; for little office
Will the hateful commons perform for us,
Except Eke curs to tear us all to pieces.
Will you go along with us?

BAGOT. No; I will to Ireland to his Majesty.
Farewell. If heart's presages be not vain,
We three here part that ne'er shall meet again.

BUSHY. That's as York thrives to beat back Bolingbroke.

GREEN. Alas, poor Duke! the task he undertakes
Is numb'ring sands and drinking oceans dry.
Where one on his side fights, thousands will fly.
Farewell at once-for once, for all, and ever.

BUSHY. Well, we may meet again.

BAGOT. I fear me, never. *Exeunt*

SCENE III

Gloucestershire

Enter BOLINGBROKE and NORTHUMBERLAND, forces

BOLINGBROKE. How far is it, my lord, to Berkeley now?

NORTHUMBERLAND. Believe me, noble lord,
I am a stranger here in Gloucestershire.
These high wild hills and rough uneven ways
Draws out our miles, and makes them wearisome;
And yet your fair discourse hath been as sugar,
Making the hard way sweet and delectable.
But I bethink me what a weary way
From Ravenspurgh to Cotswold will be found
In Ross and Willoughby, wanting your company,
Which, I protest, hath very much beguil'd
The tediousness and process of my travel.
But theirs is sweet'ned with the hope to have
The present benefit which I possess;
And hope to joy is little less in joy
Than hope enjoy'd. By this the weary lords
Shall make their way seem short, as mine hath done
By sight of what I have, your noble company.

BOLINGBROKE. Of much less value is my company
Than your good words. But who comes here?

Enter HARRY PERCY

NORTHUMBERLAND. It is my son, young Harry Percy,

Sent from my brother Worcester, whencesoever.
Harry, how fares your uncle?

PERCY. I had thought, my lord, to have learn'd his
health of you.

NORTHUMBERLAND. Why, is he not with the
Queen?

PERCY. No, my good lord; he hath forsook the court,
Broken his staff of office, and dispers'd
The household of the King.

NORTHUMBERLAND. What was his reason?
He was not so resolv'd when last we spake together.

PERCY. Because your lordship was proclaimed traitor.
But he, my lord, is gone to Ravenspurgh,
To offer service to the Duke of Hereford;
And sent me over by Berkeley, to discover
What power the Duke of York had levied there;
Then with directions to repair to Ravenspurgh.

NORTHUMBERLAND. Have you forgot the Duke of
Hereford, boy?

PERCY. No, my good lord; for that is not forgot
Which ne'er I did remember; to my knowledge,
I never in my life did look on him.

NORTHUMBERLAND. Then learn to know him now;
this is the Duke.

PERCY. My gracious lord, I tender you my service,
Such as it is, being tender, raw, and young;
Which elder days shall ripen, and confirm
To more approved service and desert.

BOLINGBROKE. I thank thee, gentle Percy; and be
sure
I count myself in nothing else so happy
As in a soul rememb'ring my good friends;
And as my fortune ripens with thy love,

It shall be still thy true love's recompense.
My heart this covenant makes, my hand thus seals it.

NORTHUMBERLAND. How far is it to Berkeley?
And what stir
Keeps good old York there with his men of war?

PERCY. There stands the castle, by yon tuft of trees,
Mann'd with three hundred men, as I have heard;
And in it are the Lords of York, Berkeley, and Seymour-
None else of name and noble estimate.

Enter ROSS and WILLOUGHBY

NORTHUMBERLAND. Here come the Lords of Ross
and Willoughby,
Bloody with spurring, fiery-red with haste.

BOLINGBROKE. Welcome, my lords. I wot your love
pursues
A banish'd traitor. All my treasury
Is yet but unfelt thanks, which, more enrich'd,
Shall be your love and labour's recompense.

ROSS. Your presence makes us rich, most noble lord.

WILLOUGHBY. And far surmounts our labour to attain
it.

BOLINGBROKE. Evermore thanks, the exchequer of
the poor;
Which, till my infant fortune comes to years,
Stands for my bounty. But who comes here?

Enter BERKELEY

NORTHUMBERLAND. It is my Lord of Berkeley, as I
guess.

BERKELEY. My Lord of Hereford, my message is to you.

BOLINGBROKE. My lord, my answer is-'to Lancaster';

And I am come to seek that name in England;
And I must find that title in your tongue
Before I make reply to aught you say.

BERKELEY. Mistake me not, my lord; 'tis not my meaning
To raze one title of your honour out.
To you, my lord, I come-what lord you will-
From the most gracious regent of this land,
The Duke of York, to know what pricks you on
To take advantage of the absent time,
And fright our native peace with self-borne arms.

Enter YORK, attended

BOLINGBROKE. I shall not need transport my words by you;
Here comes his Grace in person. My noble uncle!
[Kneels]

YORK. Show me thy humble heart, and not thy knee,
Whose duty is deceivable and false.

BOLINGBROKE. My gracious uncle!-

YORK. Tut, tut!
Grace me no grace, nor uncle me no uncle.
I am no traitor's uncle; and that word 'grace'
In an ungracious mouth is but profane.
Why have those banish'd and forbidden legs
Dar'd once to touch a dust of England's ground?
But then more 'why?'-why have they dar'd to march
So many miles upon her peaceful bosom,
Frighting her pale-fac'd villages with war
And ostentation of despised arms?
Com'st thou because the anointed King is hence?
Why, foolish boy, the King is left behind,
And in my loyal bosom lies his power.
Were I but now lord of such hot youth
As when brave Gaunt, thy father, and myself

Rescued the Black Prince, that young Mars of men,
From forth the ranks of many thousand French,
O, then how quickly should this arm of mine,
Now prisoner to the palsy, chastise the
And minister correction to thy fault!

BOLINGBROKE My gracious uncle, let me know my
fault;
On what condition stands it and wherein?

YORK. Even in condition of the worst degree-
In gross rebellion and detested treason.
Thou art a banish'd man, and here art come
Before the expiration of thy time,
In braving arms against thy sovereign.

BOLINGBROKE. As I was banish'd, I was banish'd
Hereford;
But as I come, I come for Lancaster.
And, noble uncle, I beseech your Grace
Look on my wrongs with an indifferent eye.
You are my father, for methinks in you
I see old Gaunt alive. O, then, my father,
Will you permit that I shall stand condemn'd
A wandering vagabond; my rights and royalties
Pluck'd from my arms perforce, and given away
To upstart unthrifts? Wherefore was I born?
If that my cousin king be King in England,
It must be granted I am Duke of Lancaster.
You have a son, Aumerle, my noble cousin;
Had you first died, and he been thus trod down,
He should have found his uncle Gaunt a father
To rouse his wrongs and chase them to the bay.
I am denied to sue my livery here,
And yet my letters patents give me leave.
My father's goods are all distrain'd and sold;
And these and all are all amiss employ'd.
What would you have me do? I am a subject,
And I challenge law-attorneys are denied me;

And therefore personally I lay my claim
To my inheritance of free descent.

NORTHUMBERLAND. The noble Duke hath been
too much abused.

ROSS. It stands your Grace upon to do him right.

WILLOUGHBY. Base men by his endowments are made
great.

YORK. My lords of England, let me tell you this:
I have had feeling of my cousin's wrongs,
And labour'd all I could to do him right;
But in this kind to come, in braving arms,
Be his own carver and cut out his way,
To find out right with wrong-it may not be;
And you that do abet him in this kind
Cherish rebellion, and are rebels all.

NORTHUMBERLAND. The noble Duke hath sworn
his coming is
But for his own; and for the right of that
We all have strongly sworn to give him aid;
And let him never see joy that breaks that oath!

YORK. Well, well, I see the issue of these arms.
I cannot mend it, I must needs confess,
Because my power is weak and all ill left;
But if I could, by Him that gave me life,
I would attach you all and make you stoop
Unto the sovereign mercy of the King;
But since I cannot, be it known unto you
I do remain as neuter. So, fare you well;
Unless you please to enter in the castle,
And there repose you for this night.

BOLINGBROKE. An offer, uncle, that we will accept.
But we must win your Grace to go with us
To Bristow Castle, which they say is held
By Bushy, Bagot, and their complices,
The caterpillars of the commonwealth,

Which I have sworn to weed and pluck away.

YORK. It may be I will go with you; but yet I'll pause,
For I am loath to break our country's laws.
Nor friends nor foes, to me welcome you are.
Things past redress are now with me past care.   *Exeunt*

SCENE IV

A camp in Wales

Enter EARL OF SALISBURY and a WELSH CAPTAIN

CAPTAIN. My Lord of Salisbury, we have stay'd ten
days
And hardly kept our countrymen together,
And yet we hear no tidings from the King;
Therefore we will disperse ourselves. Farewell.

SALISBURY. Stay yet another day, thou trusty
Welshman;
The King reposeth all his confidence in thee.

CAPTAIN. 'Tis thought the King is dead; we will not
stay.
The bay trees in our country are all wither'd,
And meteors fright the fixed stars of heaven;
The pale-fac'd moon looks bloody on the earth,
And lean-look'd prophets whisper fearful change;
Rich men look sad, and ruffians dance and leap-
The one in fear to lose what they enjoy,
The other to enjoy by rage and war.
These signs forerun the death or fall of kings.
Farewell. Our countrymen are gone and fled,
As well assur'd Richard their King is dead.   *Exit*

SALISBURY. Ah, Richard, with the eyes of heavy mind,
I see thy glory like a shooting star
Fall to the base earth from the firmament!

The sun sets weeping in the lowly west,
Witnessing storms to come, woe, and unrest;
Thy friends are fled, to wait upon thy foes;
And crossly to thy good all fortune goes.   *Exit*

ACT III

SCENE I

BOLINGBROKE'S camp at Bristol

Enter BOLINGBROKE, NORTHUMBERLAND, YORK, PERCY, ROSS, WILLOUGHBY, BUSHY and GREEN, prisoners

BOLINGBROKE. Bring forth these men.
Bushy and Green, I will not vex your souls-
Since presently your souls must part your bodies-
With too much urging your pernicious lives,
For 'twere no charity; yet, to wash your blood
From off my hands, here in the view of men
I will unfold some causes of your deaths:
You have misled a prince, a royal king,
A happy gentleman in blood and lineaments,
By you unhappied and disfigured clean;
You have in manner with your sinful hours
Made a divorce betwixt his queen and him;
Broke the possession of a royal bed,
And stain'd the beauty of a fair queen's cheeks
With tears drawn from her eyes by your foul wrongs;
Myself-a prince by fortune of my birth,
Near to the King in blood, and near in love
Till you did make him misinterpret me-
Have stoop'd my neck under your injuries
And sigh'd my English breath in foreign clouds,
Eating the bitter bread of banishment,
Whilst you have fed upon my signories,
Dispark'd my parks and fell'd my forest woods,
From my own windows torn my household coat,
Raz'd out my imprese, leaving me no sign
Save men's opinions and my living blood
To show the world I am a gentleman.
This and much more, much more than twice all this,

Condemns you to the death. See them delivered over
To execution and the hand of death.

BUSHY. More welcome is the stroke of death to me
Than Bolingbroke to England. Lords, farewell.

GREEN. My comfort is that heaven will take our souls,
And plague injustice with the pains of hell.

BOLINGBROKE. My Lord Northumberland, see them
dispatch'd.

*Exeunt NORTHUMBERLAND, and others, with the
prisoners*

Uncle, you say the Queen is at your house;
For God's sake, fairly let her be entreated.
Tell her I send to her my kind commends;
Take special care my greetings be delivered.

YORK. A gentleman of mine I have dispatch'd
With letters of your love to her at large.

BOLINGBROKE. Thanks, gentle uncle. Come, lords,
away,
To fight with Glendower and his complices.
Awhile to work, and after holiday.   *Exeunt*

SCENE II

The coast of Wales. A castle in view

*Drums. Flourish and colours. Enter the KING, the
BISHOP OF CARLISLE, AUMERLE, and soldiers*

KING RICHARD. Barkloughly Castle can they this at
hand?

AUMERLE. Yea, my lord. How brooks your Grace the
air
After your late tossing on the breaking seas?

KING RICHARD. Needs must I like it well. I weep for joy
To stand upon my kingdom once again.
Dear earth, I do salute thee with my hand,
Though rebels wound thee with their horses' hoofs.
As a long-parted mother with her child
Plays fondly with her tears and smiles in meeting,
So weeping-smiling greet I thee, my earth,
And do thee favours with my royal hands.
Feed not thy sovereign's foe, my gentle earth,
Nor with thy sweets comfort his ravenous sense;
But let thy spiders, that suck up thy venom,
And heavy-gaited toads, lie in their way,
Doing annoyance to the treacherous feet
Which with usurping steps do trample thee;
Yield stinging nettles to mine enemies;
And when they from thy bosom pluck a flower,
Guard it, I pray thee, with a lurking adder,
Whose double tongue may with a mortal touch
Throw death upon thy sovereign's enemies.
Mock not my senseless conjuration, lords.
This earth shall have a feeling, and these stones
Prove armed soldiers, ere her native king
Shall falter under foul rebellion's arms.

CARLISLE. Fear not, my lord; that Power that made you king
Hath power to keep you king in spite of all.
The means that heaven yields must be embrac'd
And not neglected; else, if heaven would,
And we will not, heaven's offer we refuse,
The proffered means of succour and redress.

AUMERLE. He means, my lord, that we are too remiss;
Whilst Bolingbroke, through our security,
Grows strong and great in substance and in power.

KING RICHARD. Discomfortable cousin! know'st thou not

That when the searching eye of heaven is hid,
Behind the globe, that lights the lower world,
Then thieves and robbers range abroad unseen
In murders and in outrage boldly here;
But when from under this terrestrial ball
He fires the proud tops of the eastern pines
And darts his light through every guilty hole,
Then murders, treasons, and detested sins,
The cloak of night being pluck'd from off their backs,
Stand bare and naked, trembling at themselves?
So when this thief, this traitor, Bolingbroke,
Who all this while hath revell'd in the night,
Whilst we were wand'ring with the Antipodes,
Shall see us rising in our throne, the east,
His treasons will sit blushing in his face,
Not able to endure the sight of day,
But self-affrighted tremble at his sin.
Not all the water in the rough rude sea
Can wash the balm off from an anointed king;
The breath of worldly men cannot depose
The deputy elected by the Lord.
For every man that Bolingbroke hath press'd
To lift shrewd steel against our golden crown,
God for his Richard hath in heavenly pay
A glorious angel. Then, if angels fight,
Weak men must fall; for heaven still guards the right.

Enter SALISBURY

Welcome, my lord. How far off lies your power?

SALISBURY. Nor near nor farther off, my gracious lord,
Than this weak arm. Discomfort guides my tongue,
And bids me speak of nothing but despair.
One day too late, I fear me, noble lord,
Hath clouded all thy happy days on earth.
O, call back yesterday, bid time return,
And thou shalt have twelve thousand fighting men!

To-day, to-day, unhappy day, too late,
O'erthrows thy joys, friends, fortune, and thy state;
For all the Welshmen, hearing thou wert dead,
Are gone to Bolingbroke, dispers'd, and fled.

AUMERLE. Comfort, my liege, why looks your Grace so
pale?

KING RICHARD. But now the blood of twenty thou-
sand men
Did triumph in my face, and they are fled;
And, till so much blood thither come again,
Have I not reason to look pale and dead?
All souls that will be safe, fly from my side;
For time hath set a blot upon my pride.

AUMERLE. Comfort, my liege; remember who you are.

KING RICHARD. I had forgot myself; am I not King?
Awake, thou coward majesty! thou sleepest.
Is not the King's name twenty thousand names?
Arm, arm, my name! a puny subject strikes
At thy great glory. Look not to the ground,
Ye favourites of a king; are we not high?
High be our thoughts. I know my uncle York
Hath power enough to serve our turn. But who comes
here?

Enter SCROOP

SCROOP. More health and happiness betide my liege
Than can my care-tun'd tongue deliver him.

KING RICHARD. Mine ear is open and my heart
prepar'd.
The worst is worldly loss thou canst unfold.
Say, is my kingdom lost? Why, 'twas my care,
And what loss is it to be rid of care?
Strives Bolingbroke to be as great as we?
Greater he shall not be; if he serve God,
We'll serve him too, and be his fellow so.

Revolt our subjects? That we cannot mend;
They break their faith to God as well as us.
Cry woe, destruction, ruin, and decay-
The worst is death, and death will have his day.

SCROOP. Glad am I that your Highness is so arm'd
To bear the tidings of calamity.
Like an unseasonable stormy day
Which makes the silver rivers drown their shores,
As if the world were all dissolv'd to tears,
So high above his limits swells the rage
Of Bolingbroke, covering your fearful land
With hard bright steel and hearts harder than steel.
White-beards have arm'd their thin and hairless scalps
Against thy majesty; boys, with women's voices,
Strive to speak big, and clap their female joints
In stiff unwieldy arms against thy crown;
Thy very beadsmen learn to bend their bows
Of double-fatal yew against thy state;
Yea, distaff-women manage rusty bills
Against thy seat: both young and old rebel,
And all goes worse than I have power to tell.

KING RICHARD. Too well, too well thou tell'st a tale
so in.
Where is the Earl of Wiltshire? Where is Bagot?
What is become of Bushy? Where is Green?
That they have let the dangerous enemy
Measure our confines with such peaceful steps?
If we prevail, their heads shall pay for it.
I warrant they have made peace with Bolingbroke.

SCROOP. Peace have they made with him indeed, my
lord.

KING RICHARD. O villains, vipers, damn'd without
redemption!
Dogs, easily won to fawn on any man!
Snakes, in my heart-blood warm'd, that sting my heart!
Three Judases, each one thrice worse than Judas!

William Shakespeare

Would they make peace? Terrible hell make war
Upon their spotted souls for this offence!

SCROOP. Sweet love, I see, changing his property,
Turns to the sourest and most deadly hate.
Again uncurse their souls; their peace is made
With heads, and not with hands; those whom you curse
Have felt the worst of death's destroying wound
And lie full low, grav'd in the hollow ground.

AUMERLE. Is Bushy, Green, and the Earl of Wiltshire
dead?

SCROOP. Ay, all of them at Bristow lost their heads.

AUMERLE. Where is the Duke my father with his
power?

KING RICHARD. No matter where-of comfort no
man speak.
Let's talk of graves, of worms, and epitaphs;
Make dust our paper, and with rainy eyes
Write sorrow on the bosom of the earth.
Let's choose executors and talk of wills;
And yet not so-for what can we bequeath
Save our deposed bodies to the ground?
Our lands, our lives, and an, are Bolingbroke's.
And nothing can we can our own but death
And that small model of the barren earth
Which serves as paste and cover to our bones.
For God's sake let us sit upon the ground
And tell sad stories of the death of kings:
How some have been depos'd, some slain in war,
Some haunted by the ghosts they have depos'd,
Some poison'd by their wives, some sleeping kill'd,
All murder'd-for within the hollow crown
That rounds the mortal temples of a king
Keeps Death his court; and there the antic sits,
Scoffing his state and grinning at his pomp;
Allowing him a breath, a little scene,

To monarchize, be fear'd, and kill with looks;
Infusing him with self and vain conceit,
As if this flesh which walls about our life
Were brass impregnable; and, humour'd thus,
Comes at the last, and with a little pin
Bores through his castle wall, and farewell, king!
Cover your heads, and mock not flesh and blood
With solemn reverence; throw away respect,
Tradition, form, and ceremonious duty;
For you have but mistook me all this while.
I live with bread like you, feel want,
Taste grief, need friends: subjected thus,
How can you say to me I am a king?

CARLISLE. My lord, wise men ne'er sit and wail their
woes,
But presently prevent the ways to wail.
To fear the foe, since fear oppresseth strength,
Gives, in your weakness, strength unto your foe,
And so your follies fight against yourself.
Fear and be slain-no worse can come to fight;
And fight and die is death destroying death,
Where fearing dying pays death servile breath.

AUMERLE. My father hath a power; inquire of him,
And learn to make a body of a limb.

KING RICHARD. Thou chid'st me well. Proud
Bolingbroke, I come
To change blows with thee for our day of doom.
This ague fit of fear is over-blown;
An easy task it is to win our own.
Say, Scroop, where lies our uncle with his power?
Speak sweetly, man, although thy looks be sour.

SCROOP. Men judge by the complexion of the sky
The state in inclination of the day;
So may you by my dull and heavy eye,
My tongue hath but a heavier tale to say.
I play the torturer, by small and small

To lengthen out the worst that must be spoken:
Your uncle York is join'd with Bolingbroke;
And all your northern castles yielded up,
And all your southern gentlemen in arms
Upon his party.

KING RICHARD. Thou hast said enough.
[To AUMERLE] Beshrew thee, cousin, which didst lead me forth
Of that sweet way I was in to despair!
What say you now? What comfort have we now?
By heaven, I'll hate him everlastingly
That bids me be of comfort any more.
Go to Flint Castle; there I'll pine away;
A king, woe's slave, shall kingly woe obey.
That power I have, discharge; and let them go
To ear the land that hath some hope to grow,
For I have none. Let no man speak again
To alter this, for counsel is but vain.

AUMERLE. My liege, one word.

KING RICHARD. He does me double wrong
That wounds me with the flatteries of his tongue.
Discharge my followers; let them hence away,
From Richard's night to Bolingbroke's fair day.   *Exeunt*

SCENE III

Wales. Before Flint Castle

*Enter, with drum and colours, BOLINGBROKE, YORK,
NORTHUMBERLAND, and forces*

BOLINGBROKE. So that by this intelligence we learn
The Welshmen are dispers'd; and Salisbury
Is gone to meet the King, who lately landed
With some few private friends upon this coast.

NORTHUMBERLAND. The news is very fair and
good, my lord.
Richard not far from hence hath hid his head.

YORK. It would beseem the Lord Northumberland
To say 'King Richard.' Alack the heavy day
When such a sacred king should hide his head!

NORTHUMBERLAND. Your Grace mistakes; only to
be brief,
Left I his title out.

YORK. The time hath been,
Would you have been so brief with him, he would
Have been so brief with you to shorten you,
For taking so the head, your whole head's length.

BOLINGBROKE. Mistake not, uncle, further than you
should.

YORK. Take not, good cousin, further than you should,
Lest you mistake. The heavens are over our heads.

BOLINGBROKE. I know it, uncle; and oppose not
myself
Against their will. But who comes here?

Enter PERCY

Welcome, Harry. What, will not this castle yield?

PIERCY. The castle royally is mann'd, my lord,
Against thy entrance.

BOLINGBROKE. Royally!
Why, it contains no king?

PERCY. Yes, my good lord,
It doth contain a king; King Richard lies
Within the limits of yon lime and stone;
And with him are the Lord Aumerle, Lord Salisbury,
Sir Stephen Scroop, besides a clergyman
Of holy reverence; who, I cannot learn.

NORTHUMBERLAND. O, belike it is the Bishop of Carlisle.

BOLINGBROKE. *[To NORTHUMBERLAND]* Noble lord,
Go to the rude ribs of that ancient castle;
Through brazen trumpet send the breath of parley
Into his ruin'd ears, and thus deliver:
Henry Bolingbroke
On both his knees doth kiss King Richard's hand,
And sends allegiance and true faith of heart
To his most royal person; hither come
Even at his feet to lay my arms and power,
Provided that my banishment repeal'd
And lands restor'd again be freely granted;
If not, I'll use the advantage of my power
And lay the summer's dust with showers of blood
Rain'd from the wounds of slaughtered Englishmen;
The which how far off from the mind of Bolingbroke
It is such crimson tempest should bedrench
The fresh green lap of fair King Richard's land,
My stooping duty tenderly shall show.
Go, signify as much, while here we march
Upon the grassy carpet of this plain.

[NORTHUMBERLAND advances to the Castle, with a trumpet]

Let's march without the noise of threat'ning drum,
That from this castle's tottered battlements
Our fair appointments may be well perus'd.
Methinks King Richard and myself should meet
With no less terror than the elements
Of fire and water, when their thund'ring shock
At meeting tears the cloudy cheeks of heaven.
Be he the fire, I'll be the yielding water;
The rage be his, whilst on the earth I rain
My waters-on the earth, and not on him.
March on, and mark King Richard how he looks.

Parle without, and answer within; then a flourish.

Enter on the walls, the KING, the BISHOP OF
CARLISLE, AUMERLE, SCROOP, and SALISBURY

See, see, King Richard doth himself appear,
As doth the blushing discontented sun
From out the fiery portal of the east,
When he perceives the envious clouds are bent
To dim his glory and to stain the track
Of his bright passage to the occident.

YORK. Yet he looks like a king. Behold, his eye,
As bright as is the eagle's, lightens forth
Controlling majesty. Alack, alack, for woe,
That any harm should stain so fair a show!

KING RICHARD. *[To NORTHUMBERLAND]* We are
amaz'd; and thus long have we stood
To watch the fearful bending of thy knee,
Because we thought ourself thy lawful King;
And if we be, how dare thy joints forget
To pay their awful duty to our presence?
If we be not, show us the hand of God
That hath dismiss'd us from our stewardship;
For well we know no hand of blood and bone
Can gripe the sacred handle of our sceptre,
Unless he do profane, steal, or usurp.
And though you think that all, as you have done,
Have torn their souls by turning them from us,
And we are barren and bereft of friends,
Yet know-my master, God omnipotent,
Is mustering in his clouds on our behalf
Armies of pestilence; and they shall strike
Your children yet unborn and unbegot,
That lift your vassal hands against my head
And threat the glory of my precious crown.
Tell Bolingbroke, for yon methinks he stands,
That every stride he makes upon my land

William Shakespeare

Is dangerous treason; he is come to open
The purple testament of bleeding war;
But ere the crown he looks for live in peace,
Ten thousand bloody crowns of mothers' sons
Shall ill become the flower of England's face,
Change the complexion of her maid-pale peace
To scarlet indignation, and bedew
Her pastures' grass with faithful English blood.

NORTHUMBERLAND. The King of Heaven forbid
our lord the King
Should so with civil and uncivil arms
Be rush'd upon! Thy thrice noble cousin,
Harry Bolingbroke, doth humbly kiss thy hand;
And by the honourable tomb he swears
That stands upon your royal grandsire's bones,
And by the royalties of both your bloods,
Currents that spring from one most gracious head,
And by the buried hand of warlike Gaunt,
And by the worth and honour of himself,
Comprising all that may be sworn or said,
His coming hither hath no further scope
Than for his lineal royalties, and to beg
Enfranchisement immediate on his knees;
Which on thy royal party granted once,
His glittering arms he will commend to rust,
His barbed steeds to stables, and his heart
To faithful service of your Majesty.
This swears he, as he is a prince, is just;
And as I am a gentleman I credit him.

KING RICHARD. Northumberland, say thus the King
returns:
His noble cousin is right welcome hither;
And all the number of his fair demands
Shall be accomplish'd without contradiction.
With all the gracious utterance thou hast
Speak to his gentle hearing kind commends.
[To AUMERLE] We do debase ourselves, cousin, do

we not,
To look so poorly and to speak so fair?
Shall we call back Northumberland, and send
Defiance to the traitor, and so die?

AUMERLE. No, good my lord; let's fight with gentle words
Till time lend friends, and friends their helpful swords.

KING RICHARD. O God, O God! that e'er this tongue of mine
That laid the sentence of dread banishment
On yon proud man should take it off again
With words of sooth! O that I were as great
As is my grief, or lesser than my name!
Or that I could forget what I have been!
Or not remember what I must be now!
Swell'st thou, proud heart? I'll give thee scope to beat,
Since foes have scope to beat both thee and me.

AUMERLE. Northumberland comes back from Bolingbroke.

KING RICHARD. What must the King do now? Must he submit?
The King shall do it. Must he be depos'd?
The King shall be contented. Must he lose
The name of king? A God's name, let it go.
I'll give my jewels for a set of beads,
My gorgeous palace for a hermitage,
My gay apparel for an almsman's gown,
My figur'd goblets for a dish of wood,
My sceptre for a palmer's walking staff,
My subjects for a pair of carved saints,
And my large kingdom for a little grave,
A little little grave, an obscure grave-
Or I'll be buried in the king's high way,
Some way of common trade, where subjects' feet
May hourly trample on their sovereign's head;
For on my heart they tread now whilst I live,

And buried once, why not upon my head?
Aumerle, thou weep'st, my tender-hearted cousin!
We'll make foul weather with despised tears;
Our sighs and they shall lodge the summer corn
And make a dearth in this revolting land.
Or shall we play the wantons with our woes
And make some pretty match with shedding tears?
As thus: to drop them still upon one place
Till they have fretted us a pair of graves
Within the earth; and, therein laid-there lies
Two kinsmen digg'd their graves with weeping eyes.
Would not this ill do well? Well, well, I see
I talk but idly, and you laugh at me.
Most mighty prince, my Lord Northumberland,
What says King Bolingbroke? Will his Majesty
Give Richard leave to live till Richard die?
You make a leg, and Bolingbroke says ay.

NORTHUMBERLAND. My lord, in the base court he
doth attend
To speak with you; may it please you to come down?

KING RICHARD. Down, down I come, like glist'ring
Phaethon,
Wanting the manage of unruly jades.
In the base court? Base court, where kings grow base,
To come at traitors' calls, and do them grace.
In the base court? Come down? Down, court! down,
king!
For night-owls shriek where mounting larks should sing.
                                        Exeunt from above

BOLINGBROKE. What says his Majesty?

NORTHUMBERLAND. Sorrow and grief of heart
Makes him speak fondly, like a frantic man;
Yet he is come.

Enter the KING, and his attendants, below

BOLINGBROKE. Stand all apart,
And show fair duty to his Majesty. *[He kneels down]*
My gracious lord-

KING RICHARD. Fair cousin, you debase your
princely knee
To make the base earth proud with kissing it.
Me rather had my heart might feel your love
Than my unpleas'd eye see your courtesy.
Up, cousin, up; your heart is up, I know,
[Touching his own head] Thus high at least, although
your knee be low.

BOLINGBROKE. My gracious lord, I come but for
mine own.

KING RICHARD. Your own is yours, and I am yours,
and all.

BOLINGBROKE. So far be mine, my most redoubted
lord,
As my true service shall deserve your love.

KING RICHARD. Well you deserve. They well deserve
to have
That know the strong'st and surest way to get.
Uncle, give me your hands; nay, dry your eyes:
Tears show their love, but want their remedies.
Cousin, I am too young to be your father,
Though you are old enough to be my heir.
What you will have, I'll give, and willing too;
For do we must what force will have us do.
Set on towards London. Cousin, is it so?

BOLINGBROKE. Yea, my good lord.

KING RICHARD. Then I must not say no.

Flourish. Exeunt

William Shakespeare

SCENE IV

The DUKE OF YORK's garden

Enter the QUEEN and two LADIES

QUEEN. What sport shall we devise here in this garden
To drive away the heavy thought of care?

LADY. Madam, we'll play at bowls.

QUEEN. 'Twill make me think the world is full of rubs
And that my fortune runs against the bias.

LADY. Madam, we'll dance.

QUEEN. My legs can keep no measure in delight,
When my poor heart no measure keeps in grief;
Therefore no dancing, girl; some other sport.

LADY. Madam, we'll tell tales.

QUEEN. Of sorrow or of joy?

LADY. Of either, madam.

QUEEN. Of neither, girl;
For if of joy, being altogether wanting,
It doth remember me the more of sorrow;
Or if of grief, being altogether had,
It adds more sorrow to my want of joy;
For what I have I need not to repeat,
And what I want it boots not to complain.

LADY. Madam, I'll sing.

QUEEN. 'Tis well' that thou hast cause;
But thou shouldst please me better wouldst thou weep.

LADY. I could weep, madam, would it do you good.

QUEEN. And I could sing, would weeping do me good,
And never borrow any tear of thee.

Enter a GARDENER and two SERVANTS

But stay, here come the gardeners.
Let's step into the shadow of these trees.
My wretchedness unto a row of pins,
They will talk of state, for every one doth so
Against a change: woe is forerun with woe.

QUEEN and LADIES retire

GARDENER. Go, bind thou up yon dangling
apricocks,
Which, like unruly children, make their sire
Stoop with oppression of their prodigal weight;
Give some supportance to the bending twigs.
Go thou, and Eke an executioner
Cut off the heads of too fast growing sprays
That look too lofty in our commonwealth:
All must be even in our government.
You thus employ'd, I will go root away
The noisome weeds which without profit suck
The soil's fertility from wholesome flowers.

SERVANT. Why should we, in the compass of a pale,
Keep law and form and due proportion,
Showing, as in a model, our firm estate,
When our sea-walled garden, the whole land,
Is full of weeds; her fairest flowers chok'd up,
Her fruit trees all unprun'd, her hedges ruin'd,
Her knots disordered, and her wholesome herbs
Swarming with caterpillars?

GARDENER. Hold thy peace.
He that hath suffer'd this disorder'd spring
Hath now himself met with the fall of leaf;
The weeds which his broad-spreading leaves did shelter,
That seem'd in eating him to hold him up,
Are pluck'd up root and all by Bolingbroke-
I mean the Earl of Wiltshire, Bushy, Green.

SERVANT. What, are they dead?

GARDENER. They are; and Bolingbroke
Hath seiz'd the wasteful King. O, what pity is it
That he had not so trimm'd and dress'd his land
As we this garden! We at time of year
Do wound the bark, the skin of our fruit trees,
Lest, being over-proud in sap and blood,
With too much riches it confound itself;
Had he done so to great and growing men,
They might have Ev'd to bear, and he to taste
Their fruits of duty. Superfluous branches
We lop away, that bearing boughs may live;
Had he done so, himself had home the crown,
Which waste of idle hours hath quite thrown down.

SERVANT. What, think you the King shall be deposed?

GARDENER. Depress'd he is already, and depos'd
'Tis doubt he will be. Letters came last night
To a dear friend of the good Duke of York's
That tell black tidings.

QUEEN. O, I am press'd to death through want of
speaking! *[Coming forward]*
Thou, old Adam's likeness, set to dress this garden,
How dares thy harsh rude tongue sound this unpleasing
news?
What Eve, what serpent, hath suggested the
To make a second fall of cursed man?
Why dost thou say King Richard is depos'd?
Dar'st thou, thou little better thing than earth,
Divine his downfall? Say, where, when, and how,
Cam'st thou by this ill tidings? Speak, thou wretch.

GARDENER. Pardon me, madam; little joy have
To breathe this news; yet what I say is true.
King Richard, he is in the mighty hold
Of Bolingbroke. Their fortunes both are weigh'd.
In your lord's scale is nothing but himself,
And some few vanities that make him light;
But in the balance of great Bolingbroke,

Besides himself, are all the English peers,
And with that odds he weighs King Richard down.
Post you to London, and you will find it so;
I speak no more than every one doth know.

QUEEN. Nimble mischance, that art so light of foot,
Doth not thy embassage belong to me,
And am I last that knows it? O, thou thinkest
To serve me last, that I may longest keep
Thy sorrow in my breast. Come, ladies, go
To meet at London London's King in woe.
What, was I born to this, that my sad look
Should grace the triumph of great Bolingbroke?
Gard'ner, for telling me these news of woe,
Pray God the plants thou graft'st may never grow!
Exeunt QUEEN and LADIES

GARDENER. Poor Queen, so that thy state might be
no worse,
I would my skill were subject to thy curse.
Here did she fall a tear; here in this place
I'll set a bank of rue, sour herb of grace.
Rue, even for ruth, here shortly shall be seen,
In the remembrance of a weeping queen.   *Exeunt*

ACT IV

SCENE I

Westminster Hall

*Enter, as to the Parliament, BOLINGBROKE,
AUMERLE, NORTHUMBERLAND, PERCY,
FITZWATER, SURREY, the BISHOP OF CARLISLE,
the ABBOT OF WESTMINSTER, and others; HERALD,
OFFICERS, and BAGOT*

BOLINGBROKE. Call forth Bagot.
Now, Bagot, freely speak thy mind-
What thou dost know of noble Gloucester's death;
Who wrought it with the King, and who perform'd
The bloody office of his timeless end.

BAGOT. Then set before my face the Lord Aumerle.

BOLINGBROKE. Cousin, stand forth, and look upon
that man.

BAGOT. My Lord Aumerle, I know your daring tongue
Scorns to unsay what once it hath deliver'd.
In that dead time when Gloucester's death was plotted
I heard you say 'Is not my arm of length,
That reacheth from the restful English Court
As far as Calais, to mine uncle's head?'
Amongst much other talk that very time
I heard you say that you had rather refuse
The offer of an hundred thousand crowns
Than Bolingbroke's return to England;
Adding withal, how blest this land would be
In this your cousin's death.

AUMERLE. Princes, and noble lords,
What answer shall I make to this base man?
Shall I so much dishonour my fair stars
On equal terms to give him chastisement?

Either I must, or have mine honour soil'd
With the attainder of his slanderous lips.
There is my gage, the manual seal of death
That marks thee out for hell. I say thou liest,
And will maintain what thou hast said is false
In thy heart-blood, through being all too base
To stain the temper of my knightly sword.

BOLINGBROKE. Bagot, forbear; thou shalt not take it up.

AUMERLE. Excepting one, I would he were the best
In all this presence that hath mov'd me so.

FITZWATER. If that thy valour stand on sympathy,
There is my gage, Aumerle, in gage to thine.
By that fair sun which shows me where thou stand'st,
I heard thee say, and vauntingly thou spak'st it,
That thou wert cause of noble Gloucester's death.
If thou deniest it twenty times, thou liest;
And I will turn thy falsehood to thy heart,
Where it was forged, with my rapier's point.

AUMERLE. Thou dar'st not, coward, live to see that day.

FITZWATER. Now, by my soul, I would it were this hour.

AUMERLE. Fitzwater, thou art damn'd to hell for this.

PERCY. Aumerle, thou liest; his honour is as true
In this appeal as thou art an unjust;
And that thou art so, there I throw my gage,
To prove it on thee to the extremest point
Of mortal breathing. Seize it, if thou dar'st.

AUMERLE. An if I do not, may my hands rot of
And never brandish more revengeful steel
Over the glittering helmet of my foe!

ANOTHER LORD. I task the earth to the like, for-
sworn Aumerle;
And spur thee on with fun as many lies

As may be halloa'd in thy treacherous ear
From sun to sun. There is my honour's pawn;
Engage it to the trial, if thou darest.

AUMERLE. Who sets me else? By heaven, I'll throw at all!
I have a thousand spirits in one breast
To answer twenty thousand such as you.

SURREY. My Lord Fitzwater, I do remember well
The very time Aumerle and you did talk.

FITZWATER. 'Tis very true; you were in presence then,
And you can witness with me this is true.

SURREY. As false, by heaven, as heaven itself is true.

FITZWATER. Surrey, thou liest.

SURREY. Dishonourable boy!
That lie shall lie so heavy on my sword
That it shall render vengeance and revenge
Till thou the lie-giver and that lie do he
In earth as quiet as thy father's skull.
In proof whereof, there is my honour's pawn;
Engage it to the trial, if thou dar'st.

FITZWATER. How fondly dost thou spur a forward horse!
If I dare eat, or drink, or breathe, or live,
I dare meet Surrey in a wilderness,
And spit upon him whilst I say he lies,
And lies, and lies. There is my bond of faith,
To tie thee to my strong correction.
As I intend to thrive in this new world,
Aumerle is guilty of my true appeal.
Besides, I heard the banish'd Norfolk say
That thou, Aumerle, didst send two of thy men
To execute the noble Duke at Calais.

AUMERLE. Some honest Christian trust me with a gage

That Norfolk lies. Here do I throw down this,
If he may be repeal'd to try his honour.

BOLINGBROKE. These differences shall all rest under
gage
Till Norfolk be repeal'd-repeal'd he shall be
And, though mine enemy, restor'd again
To all his lands and signories. When he is return'd,
Against Aumerle we will enforce his trial.

CARLISLE. That honourable day shall never be seen.
Many a time hath banish'd Norfolk fought
For Jesu Christ in glorious Christian field,
Streaming the ensign of the Christian cross
Against black pagans, Turks, and Saracens;
And, toil'd with works of war, retir'd himself
To Italy; and there, at Venice, gave
His body to that pleasant country's earth,
And his pure soul unto his captain, Christ,
Under whose colours he had fought so long.

BOLINGBROKE. Why, Bishop, is Norfolk dead?

CARLISLE. As surely as I live, my lord.

BOLINGBROKE. Sweet peace conduct his sweet soul
to the bosom
Of good old Abraham! Lords appellants,
Your differences shall all rest under gage
Till we assign you to your days of trial

Enter YORK, attended

YORK. Great Duke of Lancaster, I come to the
From plume-pluck'd Richard, who with willing soul
Adopts thee heir, and his high sceptre yields
To the possession of thy royal hand.
Ascend his throne, descending now from him-
And long live Henry, fourth of that name!

BOLINGBROKE. In God's name, I'll ascend the

regal throne.

CARLISLE. Marry, God forbid!
Worst in this royal presence may I speak,
Yet best beseeming me to speak the truth.
Would God that any in this noble presence
Were enough noble to be upright judge
Of noble Richard! Then true noblesse would
Learn him forbearance from so foul a wrong.
What subject can give sentence on his king?
And who sits here that is not Richard's subject?
Thieves are not judg'd but they are by to hear,
Although apparent guilt be seen in them;
And shall the figure of God's majesty,
His captain, steward, deputy elect,
Anointed, crowned, planted many years,
Be judg'd by subject and inferior breath,
And he himself not present? O, forfend it, God,
That in a Christian climate souls refin'd
Should show so heinous, black, obscene a deed!
I speak to subjects, and a subject speaks,
Stirr'd up by God, thus boldly for his king.
My Lord of Hereford here, whom you call king,
Is a foul traitor to proud Hereford's king;
And if you crown him, let me prophesy-
The blood of English shall manure the ground,
And future ages groan for this foul act;
Peace shall go sleep with Turks and infidels,
And in this seat of peace tumultuous wars
Shall kin with kin and kind with kind confound;
Disorder, horror, fear, and mutiny,
Shall here inhabit, and this land be call'd
The field of Golgotha and dead men's skulls.
O, if you raise this house against this house,
It will the woefullest division prove
That ever fell upon this cursed earth.
Prevent it, resist it, let it not be so,
Lest child, child's children, cry against you woe.

NORTHUMBERLAND. Well have you argued, sir;
and, for your pains,
Of capital treason we arrest you here.
My Lord of Westminster, be it your charge
To keep him safely till his day of trial.
May it please you, lords, to grant the commons' suit?

BOLINGBROKE. Fetch hither Richard, that in com-
mon view
He may surrender; so we shall proceed
Without suspicion.

YORK. I will be his conduct.   *Exit*

BOLINGBROKE. Lords, you that here are under our
arrest,
Procure your sureties for your days of answer.
Little are we beholding to your love,
And little look'd for at your helping hands.

*Re-enter YORK, with KING RICHARD, and OFFICERS
bearing the regalia*

KING RICHARD. Alack, why am I sent for to a king,
Before I have shook off the regal thoughts
Wherewith I reign'd? I hardly yet have learn'd
To insinuate, flatter, bow, and bend my knee.
Give sorrow leave awhile to tutor me
To this submission. Yet I well remember
The favours of these men. Were they not mine?
Did they not sometime cry 'All hail!' to me?
So Judas did to Christ; but he, in twelve,
Found truth in all but one; I, in twelve thousand, none.
God save the King! Will no man say amen?
Am I both priest and clerk? Well then, amen.
God save the King! although I be not he;
And yet, amen, if heaven do think him me.
To do what service am I sent for hither?

YORK. To do that office of thine own good will

Which tired majesty did make thee offer-
The resignation of thy state and crown
To Henry Bolingbroke.

KING RICHARD. Give me the crown. Here, cousin,
seize the crown.
Here, cousin,
On this side my hand, and on that side thine.
Now is this golden crown like a deep well
That owes two buckets, filling one another;
The emptier ever dancing in the air,
The other down, unseen, and full of water.
That bucket down and fun of tears am I,
Drinking my griefs, whilst you mount up on high.

BOLINGBROKE. I thought you had been willing to
resign.

KING RICHARD. My crown I am; but still my griefs
are mine.
You may my glories and my state depose,
But not my griefs; still am I king of those.

BOLINGBROKE. Part of your cares you give me with
your crown.

KING RICHARD. Your cares set up do not pluck my
cares down.
My care is loss of care, by old care done;
Your care is gain of care, by new care won.
The cares I give I have, though given away;
They tend the crown, yet still with me they stay.

BOLINGBROKE. Are you contented to resign the
crown?

KING RICHARD. Ay, no; no, ay; for I must nothing
be;
Therefore no no, for I resign to thee.
Now mark me how I will undo myself:
I give this heavy weight from off my head,
And this unwieldy sceptre from my hand,

The pride of kingly sway from out my heart;
With mine own tears I wash away my balm,
With mine own hands I give away my crown,
With mine own tongue deny my sacred state,
With mine own breath release all duteous oaths;
All pomp and majesty I do forswear;
My manors, rents, revenues, I forgo;
My acts, decrees, and statutes, I deny.
God pardon all oaths that are broke to me!
God keep all vows unbroke are made to thee!
Make me, that nothing have, with nothing griev'd,
And thou with all pleas'd, that hast an achiev'd.
Long mayst thou live in Richard's seat to sit,
And soon lie Richard in an earthly pit.
God save King Henry, unking'd Richard says,
And send him many years of sunshine days!
What more remains?

NORTHUMBERLAND. No more; but that you read
These accusations, and these grievous crimes
Committed by your person and your followers
Against the state and profit of this land;
That, by confessing them, the souls of men
May deem that you are worthily depos'd.

KING RICHARD. Must I do so? And must I ravel out
My weav'd-up follies? Gentle Northumberland,
If thy offences were upon record,
Would it not shame thee in so fair a troop
To read a lecture of them? If thou wouldst,
There shouldst thou find one heinous article,
Containing the deposing of a king
And cracking the strong warrant of an oath,
Mark'd with a blot, damn'd in the book of heaven.
Nay, all of you that stand and look upon me
Whilst that my wretchedness doth bait myself,
Though some of you, with Pilate, wash your hands,
Showing an outward pity-yet you Pilates
Have here deliver'd me to my sour cross,

And water cannot wash away your sin.

NORTHUMBERLAND. My lord, dispatch; read o'er these articles.

KING RICHARD. Mine eyes are full of tears; I cannot see.
And yet salt water blinds them not so much
But they can see a sort of traitors here.
Nay, if I turn mine eyes upon myself,
I find myself a traitor with the rest;
For I have given here my soul's consent
T'undeck the pompous body of a king;
Made glory base, and sovereignty a slave,
Proud majesty a subject, state a peasant.

NORTHUMBERLAND. My lord-

KING RICHARD. No lord of thine, thou haught insulting man,
Nor no man's lord; I have no name, no tide-
No, not that name was given me at the font-
But 'tis usurp'd. Alack the heavy day,
That I have worn so many winters out,
And know not now what name to call myself!
O that I were a mockery king of snow,
Standing before the sun of Bolingbroke
To melt myself away in water drops!
Good king, great king, and yet not greatly good,
An if my word be sterling yet in England,
Let it command a mirror hither straight,
That it may show me what a face I have
Since it is bankrupt of his majesty.

BOLINGBROKE. Go some of you and fetch a looking-glass.   *Exit an attendant*

NORTHUMBERLAND. Read o'er this paper while the glass doth come.

KING RICHARD. Fiend, thou torments me ere I come to hell.

BOLINGBROKE. Urge it no more, my Lord Northumberland.

NORTHUMBERLAND. The Commons will not, then, be satisfied.

KING RICHARD. They shall be satisfied. I'll read enough,
When I do see the very book indeed
Where all my sins are writ, and that's myself.

Re-enter attendant with glass

Give me that glass, and therein will I read.
No deeper wrinkles yet? Hath sorrow struck
So many blows upon this face of mine
And made no deeper wounds? O flatt'ring glass,
Like to my followers in prosperity,
Thou dost beguile me! Was this face the face
That every day under his household roof
Did keep ten thousand men? Was this the face
That like the sun did make beholders wink?
Is this the face which fac'd so many follies
That was at last out-fac'd by Bolingbroke?
A brittle glory shineth in this face;
As brittle as the glory is the face;

[Dashes the glass against the ground]

For there it is, crack'd in a hundred shivers.
Mark, silent king, the moral of this sport-
How soon my sorrow hath destroy'd my face.

BOLINGBROKE. The shadow of your sorrow hath destroy'd
The shadow of your face.

KING RICHARD. Say that again.
The shadow of my sorrow? Ha! let's see.
'Tis very true: my grief lies all within;
And these external manner of laments

Are merely shadows to the unseen grief
That swells with silence in the tortur'd soul.
There lies the substance; and I thank thee, king,
For thy great bounty, that not only giv'st
Me cause to wail, but teachest me the way
How to lament the cause. I'll beg one boon,
And then be gone and trouble you no more.
Shall I obtain it?

BOLINGBROKE. Name it, fair cousin.

KING RICHARD. Fair cousin! I am greater than a
king;
For when I was a king, my flatterers
Were then but subjects; being now a subject,
I have a king here to my flatterer.
Being so great, I have no need to beg.

BOLINGBROKE. Yet ask.

KING RICHARD. And shall I have?

BOLINGBROKE. You shall.

KING RICHARD. Then give me leave to go.

BOLINGBROKE. Whither?

KING RICHARD. Whither you will, so I were from
your sights.

BOLINGBROKE. Go, some of you convey him to the
Tower.

KING RICHARD. O, good! Convey! Conveyers are
you all,
That rise thus nimbly by a true king's fall.

Exeunt KING RICHARD, some Lords and a Guard

BOLINGBROKE. On Wednesday next we solemnly set
down
Our coronation. Lords, prepare yourselves.

Exeunt all but the ABBOT OF WESTMINSTER, the

BISHOP OF CARLISLE, and AUMERLE

ABBOT. A woeful pageant have we here beheld.

CARLISLE. The woe's to come; the children yet
unborn
Shall feel this day as sharp to them as thorn.

AUMERLE. You holy clergymen, is there no plot
To rid the realm of this pernicious blot?

ABBOT. My lord,
Before I freely speak my mind herein,
You shall not only take the sacrament
To bury mine intents, but also to effect
Whatever I shall happen to devise.
I see your brows are full of discontent,
Your hearts of sorrow, and your eyes of tears.
Come home with me to supper; I will lay
A plot shall show us all a merry day.   *Exeunt*

ACT V

SCENE I

London. A street leading to the Tower

Enter the QUEEN, with her attendants

QUEEN. This way the King will come; this is the way
To Julius Caesar's ill-erected tower,
To whose flint bosom my condemned lord
Is doom'd a prisoner by proud Bolingbroke.
Here let us rest, if this rebellious earth
Have any resting for her true King's queen.

Enter KING RICHARD and Guard

But soft, but see, or rather do not see,
My fair rose wither. Yet look up, behold,
That you in pity may dissolve to dew,
And wash him fresh again with true-love tears.
Ah, thou, the model where old Troy did stand;
Thou map of honour, thou King Richard's tomb,
And not King Richard; thou most beauteous inn,
Why should hard-favour'd grief be lodg'd in thee,
When triumph is become an alehouse guest?

KING RICHARD. Join not with grief, fair woman, do
not so,
To make my end too sudden. Learn, good soul,
To think our former state a happy dream;
From which awak'd, the truth of what we are
Shows us but this: I am sworn brother, sweet,
To grim Necessity; and he and
Will keep a league till death. Hie thee to France,
And cloister thee in some religious house.
Our holy lives must win a new world's crown,
Which our profane hours here have thrown down.

QUEEN. What, is my Richard both in shape and mind
Transform'd and weak'ned? Hath Bolingbroke depos'd
Thine intellect? Hath he been in thy heart?
The lion dying thrusteth forth his paw
And wounds the earth, if nothing else, with rage
To be o'erpow'r'd; and wilt thou, pupil-like,
Take the correction mildly, kiss the rod,
And fawn on rage with base humility,
Which art a lion and the king of beasts?

KING RICHARD. A king of beasts, indeed! If aught
but beasts,
I had been still a happy king of men.
Good sometimes queen, prepare thee hence for France.
Think I am dead, and that even here thou takest,
As from my death-bed, thy last living leave.
In winter's tedious nights sit by the fire
With good old folks, and let them tell thee tales
Of woeful ages long ago betid;
And ere thou bid good night, to quit their griefs
Tell thou the lamentable tale of me,
And send the hearers weeping to their beds;
For why, the senseless brands will sympathize
The heavy accent of thy moving tongue,
And in compassion weep the fire out;
And some will mourn in ashes, some coal-black,
For the deposing of a rightful king.

Enter NORTHUMBERLAND attended

NORTHUMBERLAND. My lord, the mind of
Bolingbroke is chang'd;
You must to Pomfret, not unto the Tower.
And, madam, there is order ta'en for you:
With all swift speed you must away to France.

KING RICHARD. Northumberland, thou ladder
wherewithal
The mounting Bolingbroke ascends my throne,

The time shall not be many hours of age
More than it is, ere foul sin gathering head
Shall break into corruption. Thou shalt think
Though he divide the realm and give thee half
It is too little, helping him to all;
And he shall think that thou, which knowest the way
To plant unrightful kings, wilt know again,
Being ne'er so little urg'd, another way
To pluck him headlong from the usurped throne.
The love of wicked men converts to fear;
That fear to hate; and hate turns one or both
To worthy danger and deserved death.

NORTHUMBERLAND. My guilt be on my head, and
there an end.
Take leave, and part; for you must part forthwith.

KING RICHARD. Doubly divorc'd! Bad men, you vio-
late
A twofold marriage—'twixt my crown and me,
And then betwixt me and my married wife.
Let me unkiss the oath 'twixt thee and me;
And yet not so, for with a kiss 'twas made.
Part us, Northumberland; I towards the north,
Where shivering cold and sickness pines the clime;
My wife to France, from whence set forth in pomp,
She came adorned hither like sweet May,
Sent back like Hallowmas or short'st of day.

QUEEN. And must we be divided? Must we part?

KING RICHARD. Ay, hand from hand, my love, and
heart from heart.

QUEEN. Banish us both, and send the King with me.

NORTHUMBERLAND. That were some love, but little
policy.

QUEEN. Then whither he goes thither let me go.

KING RICHARD. So two, together weeping, make

one woe.
Weep thou for me in France, I for thee here;
Better far off than near, be ne'er the near.
Go, count thy way with sighs; I mine with groans.

QUEEN. So longest way shall have the longest moans.

KING RICHARD. Twice for one step I'll groan, the
way being short,
And piece the way out with a heavy heart.
Come, come, in wooing sorrow let's be brief,
Since, wedding it, there is such length in grief.
One kiss shall stop our mouths, and dumbly part;
Thus give I mine, and thus take I thy heart.

QUEEN. Give me mine own again; 'twere no good part
To take on me to keep and kill thy heart.
So, now I have mine own again, be gone.
That I may strive to kill it with a groan.

KING RICHARD. We make woe wanton with this
fond delay.
Once more, adieu; the rest let sorrow say.   *Exeunt*

SCENE II

The DUKE OF YORK's palace

Enter the DUKE OF YORK and the DUCHESS

DUCHESS. My Lord, you told me you would tell the
rest,
When weeping made you break the story off,
Of our two cousins' coming into London.

YORK. Where did I leave?

DUCHESS. At that sad stop, my lord,
Where rude misgoverned hands from windows' tops
Threw dust and rubbish on King Richard's head.

William Shakespeare

YORK. Then, as I said, the Duke, great Bolingbroke,
Mounted upon a hot and fiery steed
Which his aspiring rider seem'd to know,
With slow but stately pace kept on his course,
Whilst all tongues cried 'God save thee, Bolingbroke!'
You would have thought the very windows spake,
So many greedy looks of young and old
Through casements darted their desiring eyes
Upon his visage; and that all the walls
With painted imagery had said at once
'Jesu preserve thee! Welcome, Bolingbroke!'
Whilst he, from the one side to the other turning,
Bareheaded, lower than his proud steed's neck,
Bespake them thus, 'I thank you, countrymen.'
And thus still doing, thus he pass'd along.

DUCHESS. Alack, poor Richard! where rode he the whilst?

YORK. As in a theatre the eyes of men
After a well-grac'd actor leaves the stage
Are idly bent on him that enters next,
Thinking his prattle to be tedious;
Even so, or with much more contempt, men's eyes
Did scowl on gentle Richard; no man cried 'God save him!'
No joyful tongue gave him his welcome home;
But dust was thrown upon his sacred head;
Which with such gentle sorrow he shook off,
His face still combating with tears and smiles,
The badges of his grief and patience,
That had not God, for some strong purpose, steel'd
The hearts of men, they must perforce have melted,
And barbarism itself have pitied him.
But heaven hath a hand in these events,
To whose high will we bound our calm contents.
To Bolingbroke are we sworn subjects now,
Whose state and honour I for aye allow.

DUCHESS. Here comes my son Aumerle.

YORK. Aumerle that was
But that is lost for being Richard's friend,
And madam, you must call him Rudand now.
I am in Parliament pledge for his truth
And lasting fealty to the new-made king.

Enter AUMERLE

DUCHESS. Welcome, my son. Who are the violets now
That strew the green lap of the new come spring?

AUMERLE. Madam, I know not, nor I greatly care not.
God knows I had as lief be none as one.

YORK. Well, bear you well in this new spring of time,
Lest you be cropp'd before you come to prime.
What news from Oxford? Do these justs and triumphs hold?

AUMERLE. For aught I know, my lord, they do.

YORK. You will be there, I know.

AUMERLE. If God prevent not, I purpose so.

YORK. What seal is that that without thy bosom?
Yea, look'st thou pale? Let me see the writing.

AUMERLE. My lord, 'tis nothing.

YORK. No matter, then, who see it.
I will be satisfied; let me see the writing.

AUMERLE. I do beseech your Grace to pardon me;
It is a matter of small consequence
Which for some reasons I would not have seen.

YORK. Which for some reasons, sir, I mean to see.
I fear, I fear-

DUCHESS. What should you fear?

'Tis nothing but some bond that he is ent'red into
For gay apparel 'gainst the triumph-day.

YORK. Bound to himself! What doth he with a bond
That he is bound to? Wife, thou art a fool.
Boy, let me see the writing.

AUMERLE. I do beseech you, pardon me; I may not
show it.

YORK. I will be satisfied; let me see it, I say.

[He plucks it out of his bosom, and reads it]

Treason, foul treason! Villain! traitor! slave!

DUCHESS. What is the matter, my lord?

YORK. Ho! who is within there?

Enter a servant

Saddle my horse.
God for his mercy, what treachery is here!

DUCHESS. Why, York, what is it, my lord?

YORK. Give me my boots, I say; saddle my horse.

Exit servant

Now, by mine honour, by my life, my troth,
I will appeach the villain.

DUCHESS. What is the matter?

YORK. Peace, foolish woman.

DUCHESS. I will not peace. What is the matter,
Aumerle?

AUMERLE. Good mother, be content; it is no more
Than my poor life must answer.

DUCHESS. Thy life answer!

YORK. Bring me my boots. I will unto the King.

His man enters with his boots

DUCHESS. Strike him, Aumerle. Poor boy, thou art amaz'd.
Hence, villain! never more come in my sight.

YORK. Give me my boots, I say.

DUCHESS. Why, York, what wilt thou do?
Wilt thou not hide the trespass of thine own?
Have we more sons? or are we like to have?
Is not my teeming date drunk up with time?
And wilt thou pluck my fair son from mine age
And rob me of a happy mother's name?
Is he not like thee? Is he not thine own?

YORK. Thou fond mad woman,
Wilt thou conceal this dark conspiracy?
A dozen of them here have ta'en the sacrament,
And interchangeably set down their hands
To kill the King at Oxford.

DUCHESS. He shall be none;
We'll keep him here. Then what is that to him?

YORK. Away, fond woman! were he twenty times my son
I would appeach him.

DUCHESS. Hadst thou groan'd for him
As I have done, thou wouldst be more pitiful.
But now I know thy mind: thou dost suspect
That I have been disloyal to thy bed
And that he is a bastard, not thy son.
Sweet York, sweet husband, be not of that mind.
He is as like thee as a man may be
Not like to me, or any of my kin,
And yet I love him.

YORK. Make way, unruly woman! *Exit*

DUCHESS. After, Aumerle! Mount thee upon his horse;

Spur post, and get before him to the King,
And beg thy pardon ere he do accuse thee.
I'll not be long behind; though I be old,
I doubt not but to ride as fast as York;
And never will I rise up from the ground
Till Bolingbroke have pardon'd thee. Away, be gone.

Exeunt

SCENE III

Windsor Castle

*Enter BOLINGBROKE as King, PERCY, and other
LORDS*

BOLINGBROKE. Can no man tell me of my unthrifty
son?
'Tis full three months since I did see him last.
If any plague hang over us, 'tis he.
I would to God, my lords, he might be found.
Inquire at London, 'mongst the taverns there,
For there, they say, he daily doth frequent
With unrestrained loose companions,
Even such, they say, as stand in narrow lanes
And beat our watch and rob our passengers,
Which he, young wanton and effeminate boy,
Takes on the point of honour to support
So dissolute a crew.

PERCY. My lord, some two days since I saw the Prince,
And told him of those triumphs held at Oxford.

BOLINGBROKE. And what said the gallant?

PERCY. His answer was, he would unto the stews,
And from the common'st creature pluck a glove
And wear it as a favour; and with that
He would unhorse the lustiest challenger.

BOLINGBROKE. As dissolute as desperate; yet through both
I see some sparks of better hope, which elder years
May happily bring forth. But who comes here?

Enter AUMERLE amazed

AUMERLE. Where is the King?

BOLINGBROKE. What means our cousin that he stares and looks
So wildly?

AUMERLE. God save your Grace! I do beseech your Majesty,
To have some conference with your Grace alone.

BOLINGBROKE. Withdraw yourselves, and leave us here alone.   *Exeunt PERCY and LORDS*
What is the matter with our cousin now?

AUMERLE. For ever may my knees grow to the earth,

[Kneels]

My tongue cleave to my roof within my mouth,
Unless a pardon ere I rise or speak.

BOLINGBROKE. Intended or committed was this fault?
If on the first, how heinous e'er it be,
To win thy after-love I pardon thee.

AUMERLE. Then give me leave that I may turn the key,
That no man enter till my tale be done.

BOLINGBROKE. Have thy desire.

[The DUKE OF YORK knocks at the door and crieth]

YORK. *[Within]* My liege, beware; look to thyself;
Thou hast a traitor in thy presence there.

BOLINGBROKE. *[Drawing]* Villain, I'll make thee safe.

AUMERLE. Stay thy revengeful hand; thou hast no cause
to fear.

YORK. *[Within]* Open the door, secure, foolhardy
King.
Shall I, for love, speak treason to thy face?
Open the door, or I will break it open.

Enter YORK

BOLINGBROKE. What is the matter, uncle? Speak;
Recover breath; tell us how near is danger,
That we may arm us to encounter it.

YORK. Peruse this writing here, and thou shalt know
The treason that my haste forbids me show.

AUMERLE. Remember, as thou read'st, thy promise
pass'd.
I do repent me; read not my name there;
My heart is not confederate with my hand.

YORK. It was, villain, ere thy hand did set it down.
I tore it from the traitor's bosom, King;
Fear, and not love, begets his penitence.
Forget to pity him, lest thy pity prove
A serpent that will sting thee to the heart.

BOLINGBROKE. O heinous, strong, and bold con-
spiracy!
O loyal father of a treacherous son!
Thou sheer, immaculate, and silver fountain,
From whence this stream through muddy passages
Hath held his current and defil'd himself!
Thy overflow of good converts to bad;
And thy abundant goodness shall excuse
This deadly blot in thy digressing son.

YORK. So shall my virtue be his vice's bawd;
And he shall spend mine honour with his shame,

As thriftless sons their scraping fathers' gold.
Mine honour lives when his dishonour dies,
Or my sham'd life in his dishonour lies.
Thou kill'st me in his life; giving him breath,
The traitor lives, the true man's put to death.

DUCHESS. *[Within]* I What ho, my liege, for God's sake, let me in.

BOLINGBROKE. What shrill-voic'd suppliant makes this eager cry?

DUCHESS. *[Within]* A woman, and thine aunt, great King; 'tis I.
Speak with me, pity me, open the door.
A beggar begs that never begg'd before.

BOLINGBROKE. Our scene is alt'red from a serious thing,
And now chang'd to 'The Beggar and the King.'
My dangerous cousin, let your mother in.
I know she is come to pray for your foul sin.

YORK. If thou do pardon whosoever pray,
More sins for this forgiveness prosper may.
This fest'red joint cut off, the rest rest sound;
This let alone will all the rest confound.

Enter DUCHESS

DUCHESS. O King, believe not this hard-hearted man!
Love loving not itself, none other can.

YORK. Thou frantic woman, what dost thou make here?
Shall thy old dugs once more a traitor rear?

DUCHESS. Sweet York, be patient. Hear me, gentle liege. *[Kneels]*

BOLINGBROKE. Rise up, good aunt.

DUCHESS. Not yet, I thee beseech.

For ever will I walk upon my knees,
And never see day that the happy sees
Till thou give joy; until thou bid me joy
By pardoning Rutland, my transgressing boy.

AUMERLE. Unto my mother's prayers I bend my knee.

[Kneels]

YORK. Against them both, my true joints bended be.

[Kneels]

Ill mayst thou thrive, if thou grant any grace!

DUCHESS. Pleads he in earnest? Look upon his face;
His eyes do drop no tears, his prayers are in jest;
His words come from his mouth, ours from our breast.
He prays but faintly and would be denied;
We pray with heart and soul, and all beside.
His weary joints would gladly rise, I know;
Our knees still kneel till to the ground they grow.
His prayers are full of false hypocrisy;
Ours of true zeal and deep integrity.
Our prayers do out-pray his; then let them have
That mercy which true prayer ought to have.

BOLINGBROKE. Good aunt, stand up.

DUCHESS. do not say 'stand up';
Say 'pardon' first, and afterwards 'stand up.'
An if I were thy nurse, thy tongue to teach,
'Pardon' should be the first word of thy speech.
I never long'd to hear a word till now;
Say 'pardon,' King; let pity teach thee how.
The word is short, but not so short as sweet;
No word like 'pardon' for kings' mouths so meet.

YORK. Speak it in French, King, say 'pardonne moy.'

DUCHESS. Dost thou teach pardon pardon to destroy?
Ah, my sour husband, my hard-hearted lord,
That sets the word itself against the word!

Speak 'pardon' as 'tis current in our land;
The chopping French we do not understand.
Thine eye begins to speak, set thy tongue there;
Or in thy piteous heart plant thou thine ear,
That hearing how our plaints and prayers do pierce,
Pity may move thee 'pardon' to rehearse.

BOLINGBROKE. Good aunt, stand up.

DUCHESS. I do not sue to stand;
Pardon is all the suit I have in hand.

BOLINGBROKE. I pardon him, as God shall pardon
me.

DUCHESS. O happy vantage of a kneeling knee!
Yet am I sick for fear. Speak it again.
Twice saying 'pardon' doth not pardon twain,
But makes one pardon strong.

BOLINGBROKE. With all my heart
I pardon him.

DUCHESS. A god on earth thou art.

BOLINGBROKE. But for our trusty brother-in-law
and the Abbot,
With all the rest of that consorted crew,
Destruction straight shall dog them at the heels.
Good uncle, help to order several powers
To Oxford, or where'er these traitors are.
They shall not live within this world, I swear,
But I will have them, if I once know where.
Uncle, farewell; and, cousin, adieu;
Your mother well hath pray'd, and prove you true.

DUCHESS. Come, my old son; I pray God make thee
new.   *Exeunt*

SCENE IV

Windsor Castle

Enter SIR PIERCE OF EXTON and a SERVANT

EXTON. Didst thou not mark the King, what words he
spake?
'Have I no friend will rid me of this living fear?'
Was it not so?

SERVANT. These were his very words.

EXTON. 'Have I no friend?' quoth he. He spake it
twice
And urg'd it twice together, did he not?

SERVANT. He did.

EXTON. And, speaking it, he wishtly look'd on me,
As who should say 'I would thou wert the man
That would divorce this terror from my heart';
Meaning the King at Pomfret. Come, let's go.
I am the King's friend, and will rid his foe.   *Exeu*nt

SCENE V

Pomfret Castle. The dungeon of the Castle

Enter KING RICHARD

KING RICHARD. I have been studying how I may
compare
This prison where I live unto the world
And, for because the world is populous
And here is not a creature but myself,
I cannot do it. Yet I'll hammer it out.
My brain I'll prove the female to my soul,
My soul the father; and these two beget

A generation of still-breeding thoughts,
And these same thoughts people this little world,
In humours like the people of this world,
For no thought is contented. The better sort,
As thoughts of things divine, are intermix'd
With scruples, and do set the word itself
Against the word,
As thus: 'Come, little ones'; and then again,
'It is as hard to come as for a camel
To thread the postern of a small needle's eye.'
Thoughts tending to ambition, they do plot
Unlikely wonders: how these vain weak nails
May tear a passage through the flinty ribs
Of this hard world, my ragged prison walls;
And, for they cannot, die in their own pride.
Thoughts tending to content flatter themselves
That they are not the first of fortune's slaves,
Nor shall not be the last; like silly beggars
Who, sitting in the stocks, refuge their shame,
That many have and others must sit there;
And in this thought they find a kind of ease,
Bearing their own misfortunes on the back
Of such as have before endur'd the like.
Thus play I in one person many people,
And none contented. Sometimes am I king;
Then treasons make me wish myself a beggar,
And so I am. Then crushing penury
Persuades me I was better when a king;
Then am I king'd again; and by and by
Think that I am unking'd by Bolingbroke,
And straight am nothing. But whate'er I be,
Nor I, nor any man that but man is,
With nothing shall be pleas'd till he be eas'd
With being nothing. *[The music plays]*
Music do I hear?
Ha, ha! keep time. How sour sweet music is
When time is broke and no proportion kept!
So is it in the music of men's lives.

William Shakespeare

And here have I the daintiness of ear
To check time broke in a disorder'd string;
But, for the concord of my state and time,
Had not an ear to hear my true time broke.
I wasted time, and now doth time waste me;
For now hath time made me his numb'ring clock:
My thoughts are minutes; and with sighs they jar
Their watches on unto mine eyes, the outward watch,
Whereto my finger, like a dial's point,
Is pointing still, in cleansing them from tears.
Now sir, the sound that tells what hour it is
Are clamorous groans which strike upon my heart,
Which is the bell. So sighs, and tears, and groans,
Show minutes, times, and hours; but my time
Runs posting on in Bolingbroke's proud joy,
While I stand fooling here, his Jack of the clock.
This music mads me. Let it sound no more;
For though it have holp madmen to their wits,
In me it seems it will make wise men mad.
Yet blessing on his heart that gives it me!
For 'tis a sign of love; and love to Richard
Is a strange brooch in this all-hating world.

Enter a GROOM of the stable

GROOM. Hail, royal Prince!

KING RICHARD. Thanks, noble peer!
The cheapest of us is ten groats too dear.
What art thou? and how comest thou hither,
Where no man never comes but that sad dog
That brings me food to make misfortune live?

GROOM. I was a poor groom of thy stable, King,
When thou wert king; who, travelling towards York,
With much ado at length have gotten leave
 To look upon my sometimes royal master's face.
O, how it ern'd my heart, when I beheld,
In London streets, that coronation-day,

When Bolingbroke rode on roan Barbary-
That horse that thou so often hast bestrid,
That horse that I so carefully have dress'd!

KING RICHARD. Rode he on Barbary? Tell me, gentle friend,
How went he under him?

GROOM. So proudly as if he disdain'd the ground.

KING RICHARD. So proud that Bolingbroke was on his back!
That jade hath eat bread from my royal hand;
This hand hath made him proud with clapping him.
Would he not stumble? would he not fall down,
Since pride must have a fall, and break the neck
Of that proud man that did usurp his back?
Forgiveness, horse! Why do I rail on thee,
Since thou, created to be aw'd by man,
Wast born to bear? I was not made a horse;
And yet I bear a burden like an ass,
Spurr'd, gall'd, and tir'd, by jauncing Bolingbroke.

Enter KEEPER with meat

KEEPER. Fellow, give place; here is no longer stay.

KING RICHARD. If thou love me, 'tis time thou wert away.

GROOM. my tongue dares not, that my heart shall say.

Exit

KEEPER. My lord, will't please you to fall to?

KING RICHARD. Taste of it first as thou art wont to do.

KEEPER. My lord, I dare not. Sir Pierce of Exton,
Who lately came from the King, commands the contrary.

KING RICHARD. The devil take Henry of Lancaster

and thee!
Patience is stale, and I am weary of it.

[Beats the KEEPER]

KEEPER. Help, help, help!

[The murderers, EXTON and servants, rush in, armed]

KING RICHARD. How now! What means death in
this rude assault?
Villain, thy own hand yields thy death's instrument.

[Snatching a weapon and killing one]

Go thou and fill another room in hell.

[He kills another, then EXTON strikes him down]

That hand shall burn in never-quenching fire
That staggers thus my person. Exton, thy fierce hand
Hath with the King's blood stain'd the King's own land.
Mount, mount, my soul! thy seat is up on high;
Whilst my gross flesh sinks downward, here to die.

[Dies]

EXTON. As full of valour as of royal blood.
Both have I spill'd. O, would the deed were good!
For now the devil, that told me I did well,
Says that this deed is chronicled in hell.
This dead King to the living King I'll bear.
Take hence the rest, and give them burial here.   *Exeunt*

SCENE VI

Windsor Castle

*Flourish. Enter BOLINGBROKE, the DUKE OF YORK,
With other LORDS and attendants*

BOLINGBROKE. Kind uncle York, the latest news

we hear
Is that the rebels have consum'd with fire
Our town of Ciceter in Gloucestershire;
But whether they be ta'en or slain we hear not.

Enter NORTHUMBERLAND

Welcome, my lord. What is the news?

NORTHUMBERLAND. First, to thy sacred state wish
I all happiness.
The next news is, I have to London sent
The heads of Salisbury, Spencer, Blunt, and Kent.
The manner of their taking may appear
At large discoursed in this paper here.

BOLINGBROKE. We thank thee, gentle Percy, for thy
pains;
And to thy worth will add right worthy gains.

Enter FITZWATER

FITZWATER. My lord, I have from Oxford sent to
London
The heads of Brocas and Sir Bennet Seely;
Two of the dangerous consorted traitors
That sought at Oxford thy dire overthrow.

BOLINGBROKE. Thy pains, Fitzwater, shall not be
forgot;
Right noble is thy merit, well I wot.

Enter PERCY, With the BISHOP OF CARLISLE

PERCY. The grand conspirator, Abbot of Westminster,
With clog of conscience and sour melancholy,
Hath yielded up his body to the grave;
But here is Carlisle living, to abide
Thy kingly doom, and sentence of his pride.

BOLINGBROKE. Carlisle, this is your doom:
Choose out some secret place, some reverend room,
More than thou hast, and with it joy thy life;
So as thou liv'st in peace, die free from strife;
For though mine enemy thou hast ever been,
High sparks of honour in thee have I seen.

Enter EXTON, with attendants, bearing a coffin

EXTON. Great King, within this coffin I present
Thy buried fear. Herein all breathless lies
The mightiest of thy greatest enemies,
Richard of Bordeaux, by me hither brought.

BOLINGBROKE. Exton, I thank thee not; for thou
hast wrought
A deed of slander with thy fatal hand
Upon my head and all this famous land.

EXTON. From your own mouth, my lord, did I this
deed.

BOLINGBROKE. They love not poison that do poison
need,
Nor do I thee. Though I did wish him dead,
I hate the murderer, love him murdered.
The guilt of conscience take thou for thy labour,
But neither my good word nor princely favour;
With Cain go wander thorough shades of night,
And never show thy head by day nor light.
Lords, I protest my soul is full of woe
That blood should sprinkle me to make me grow.
Come, mourn with me for what I do lament,
And put on sullen black incontinent.
I'll make a voyage to the Holy Land,
To wash this blood off from my guilty hand.
March sadly after; grace my mournings here
In weeping after this untimely bier.   *Exeunt*